# Interpreting
# the Book
# of Revelation

## J. Ramsey Michaels

Baker Books

A Division of Baker Book House Co
Grand Rapids, Michigan 49516

Published by Baker Books
a division of Baker Book House Company
P. O. Box 6287, Grand Rapids, MI 49516-6287

*Second printing, July 1995*

Printed in the United States of America

**Library of Congress Cataloging-in-Publication Data**

Michaels, J. Ramsey
    Interpreting the Book of Revelation / J. Ramsey Michaels.
        p.    cm.    — (Guides to New Testament Exegesis ; 7 [formerly 6])
    Includes bibliographical references.
    ISBN 0-8010-6293-4
    1. Bible. N.T. Revelation—Criticism, interpretation, etc.
I. Title. II. Series.
BS2825.2.M533  1992
228'.06—dc20                                          92-16597

All Scripture quotations are the author's translation.

# Contents

Editor's Preface  7
Author's Preface  9
Introduction  13

**Part 1    General Considerations in the Exegesis
        of Revelation**

1   Genre and Authorship  21
2   Historical and Social Setting  35
3   Problems of Structure  51

**Part 2    Specific Examples of Exegesis in Revelation**

4   Text Criticism  75
5   Grammar and Style  85
6   Narrative Criticism: The Voices of the Revelation  95
7   Tradition History: Images Transformed  107
8   Theological Interpretation: The Horizons of Patmos  129

Select Bibliography for the Book of Revelation  149

91506

# Editor's Preface

Four literary types (genres) comprise the New Testament: the Gospels, the Acts of the Apostles, the Letters, and, finally, the Apocalypse. Each genre is distinct, and, as has been made abundantly clear by contemporary scholars, each requires different sensitivities, principles, and methods of interpretation. Consequently, applying the same method to different genres will often lead to serious misunderstandings. Consequently, students need manuals that will introduce them both to the specific nature of a particular genre and to basic principles for exegeting that genre.

The Guides to New Testament Exegesis series has specifically been designed to meet this need. These guides have been written, not for specialists, but for college religion majors, seminarians, and pastors who have had at least one year of Greek. Methods and principles may change, but the language of the New Testament remains the same. God chose to speak to people in Greek; serious students of the New Testament must learn to love that language in order to better understand the Word of God.

These guides also have a practical aim. Each guide presents various views of scholars on particular issues. Yet the ultimate goal of each is to provide methods and principles for interpreting the New Testament. Abstract discussions have their proper place, but not in this series; these guides are intended for concrete application to the New Testament text. Various scholars, specializing in given areas of New Testament study, offer students their own methods and principles for interpreting specific genres of the New Testament. Such diversity provides a broader perspective for the student. Each volume concludes with a bibliography or appendix recommending works for further study.

Previously the point was made that different genres require different methods and principles. A basic exegetical method that can be adapted to various genres, however, is also essential. Because of the inevitable overlap of procedures, an introductory volume to the series covers the basic methods and principles for each genre. The individual exegetical guides will then introduce the student to more specific background procedures for that particular genre.

The vision for this series comes from Gordon Fee's introduction to New Testament exegesis.[1] Without minimizing the important contribution Fee has made to New Testament study, this series goes beyond what he has presented. It intends to develop, as it were, handbooks for each of the genres of the New Testament.[2]

Finally, this series is dedicated to our teachers and students, in thanksgiving and hope. Our prayer is that God may use these books to lead his people into truth, love, and peace.

*Scot McKnight*

---

1. New Testament Exegesis: A Handbook for Students and Pastors (Philadelphia: Westminster, 1983).

2. A helpful introduction to the various genres of the New Testament is David E. Aune, *The New Testament in Its Literary Environment*, Library of Early Christianity (Philadelphia: Westminster, 1987).

# Author's Preface

This book is the product of a sabbatical in Cambridge, England, in the winter and spring of 1991. The setting was idyllic, even in winter, yet strangely apocalyptic, like the Book of Revelation itself. The "Gulf War" between the United Nations forces and Iraq broke out two weeks after Betty and I arrived in Cambridge. We were awakened one night by a telephone call from our son in Boston, telling us that Saddam Hussein had just bombed Tel Aviv. The pages I wrote during those uncertain days from January to April will always be linked in my mind to the Middle East and the crisis in the Gulf. I finished the manuscript during a period in April when Betty was back in the United States helping out with the birth of our seventh grandchild, Michael Julian.

Long before that, friends had smiled knowingly when I said I would be writing a book on Revelation. Would I have light to shed on Saddam and his intentions, on the fate of Israel, or on the time of Christ's return? As the Gulf War progressed, even I mused about Isaiah's messianic figure coming "from Bozrah in garments stained crimson" (Isa. 63:1) and—in words remembered from another time—"trampling out the vintage where the grapes of wrath are stored." Yet I knew that whatever light my book might shed on the crisis of the moment, it would not be exactly what my friends—and many other Americans—had in mind.

Interpreting biblical prophecy is more complex, and yet in a strange way more simple, than we suppose. What the Book of Revelation requires is not that we know in advance what is coming, but that we know how to meet it when it comes (see Rev. 13:10; 14:12).

All the author asks is that we, his readers, stand beside him in his visions, see what he saw, hear what he heard, and share his wonder at things even he did not fully understand. This is what I want to help my readers do in this brief guide.

I thank my colleagues in religious studies, as well as the administration and trustees, at Southwest Missouri State University for making the half-year sabbatical possible. I also thank the staff at Tyndale House in Cambridge, who provided a quiet haven, richly stocked with the resources I needed, and an atmosphere of Christian warmth and friendship. Many new friends in Cambridge welcomed us and helped, more than they know, to make our stay happy and productive. Above all, I am grateful to my wife Betty for those days of work, play, love, and reflection we shared. With her I dedicate this volume to our children and grandchildren, the whole clan—to Carolyn, Linda, David, and Ken; to William, Renee, Luke, Stephen, Grace, Kyle, and Michael Julian—and to the future.

J. Ramsey Michaels

For thou hast laid a mighty treasure by
Unlocked by Him in Nature, and thine eye
Burns with a vision and apocalypse
Thy own sweet soul can hardly understand.

George MacDonald, "The Beloved Disciple"
*The Poetical Works of George MacDonald*,
2 vols. (London: Chatto and Windus, 1911), 2:304.

# Introduction

Two young candidates, just beginning their Ph.D. studies in mathematics, were invited to attend the annual meeting of a learned society. As they listened to an extremely complex and abstract lecture on some aspect of mathematical logic, one asked the other, "Do you understand what she's saying?" "Yes," was the reply, "I understand what she's saying. I just don't know what she's saying it about."

The student of the Book of Revelation naturally wants to know both what the last book of the Bible is saying and what it is saying it about. The purpose of this guidebook is to provide the student with some help in those tasks. All but two of the chapters in this volume are addressed to the simple—though by no means easy—question of what the Book of Revelation is saying. Chapters 2 and 8 (in very different ways) tackle the more formidable issue of what the Book of Revelation is about.

The latter question is the one that interests the general public and probably led the student to the Book of Revelation in the first place. Various answers to that question have been given. The first, naive, answer is that the Book of Revelation concerns the actual future of the world in which we live, and that alone. It was written to make known "what must happen soon" (Rev. 1:1). This is the answer with which many students have grown up, the answer they heard from Bible believing parents or preachers or from television evangelists. They may even have heard it from a secular mass media fascinated with the number 666 (Rev. 13:18) in relation to witchcraft and the occult, and with the battle of Armageddon (Rev. 16:16) in relation to current world crises. A second, more scholarly, answer is that the

Book of Revelation describes the past, not the future, specifically a conflict taking place in the author's own time between Christians in Asia Minor and the imperial power of ancient Rome. A third answer, one favored by many evangelical students and their teachers, is that the Book of Revelation refers *both* to a late-first-century crisis between Christians and the Roman Empire *and* to a last or "eschatological" crisis just before the end of the present world order and the second coming of Jesus Christ. A fourth answer is that the Book of Revelation refers *neither* to past nor future events, that it is not "about" anything at all, except what was going on in the mind of the author and the apocalyptic community to which the author belonged.

Whether the Book of Revelation is about the future or the past, or both, or neither, the question of the reality to which it refers cannot be avoided and will not be avoided in this guidebook. Because of this question, raised in a variety of ways by current events and the media, the Revelation has become for many a port of entry to the study of the whole Bible. Unfortunately, many Christians otherwise equipped to guide inquirers spiritually are neither prepared nor inclined to answer blunt questions about the meaning of this text. One reason is that Revelation is not exactly typical of the books of the New Testament. Nothing in the rest of the New Testament quite prepares us for what we find there. The student who has worked carefully through other volumes of the Guides to New Testament Exegesis series is only partially ready to interpret the Revelation. Another reason is that Revelation has fallen, time and again, into the hands of irresponsible interpreters more interested in playing on the fears and hatreds of their own time than in an honest and sober involvement with the text. Nowhere is W. B. Yeats' lament that "the best lack all conviction while the worst are full of passionate intensity" more apt than in the study of this book.

Still, a number of things learned from the rest of the Bible *are* helpful and important in approaching the Book of Revelation. Anyone who supposes that we enter here a totally different world surely has not been paying attention. Like the letters of Paul, Revelation is a letter; like the Gospels and Acts, it is full of narrative. In the Gospels, however, the narrator remains anonymous, while here the narratives are personal in that the narrator identifies himself by name (Rev. 1:9, 22:8) and consistently speaks as "I." In this respect the narratives are comparable to Paul's account of his life in Galatians 1:11–2:14, or the speeches attributed to Paul in Acts 22:3–21 and 26:4–23. These narratives also relate visions. Whatever else can be said about its genre, the Book of Revelation presents itself as one man's testimony to what he saw (Rev. 1:2).

The best way for a student of the New Testament to learn what to expect from the Book of Revelation is to look at such passages as the last discourse of Jesus, recorded in Mark 13 and paralleled in Matthew 24 and Luke 21, and certain sections of Paul's letters, above all 1 Thessalonians 4:13–18, 2 Thessalonians 2:1–12, and 1 Corinthians 15:20–26, 51–53. These passages show that Jesus and all the New Testament writers shared an expectation that the kingdom of God (Mark 1:15), or "our salvation" (Rom. 13:11), or the "end of all things" (1 Pet. 4:11), or "the Lord's coming" (James 5:8) was near. The passages also express a common desire for sequence in the plan of God, a concern about what to look for first. They exhibit a character usually described as *apocalyptic*, precisely because of the similarity to the Book of Revelation itself, traditionally known as *the Apocalypse* (Rev. 1:1).

To make sense of the Book of Revelation the student must try to understand, and even cultivate, the apocalyptic frame of mind. This means putting away certain twentieth-century biases and reserving judgment about the religious experiences that underlie this book and the images with which it is filled. Nothing is gained except wordiness by saying "John claimed to have seen an angel" instead of "John saw an angel" or "John thought he was caught up to heaven" instead of "John was caught up to heaven." A certain suspension of disbelief helps the reader understand the Book of Revelation, just as it helps with the understanding of such Old Testament books as Ezekiel or Daniel, or with the apocalyptic literature of early Judaism (see chapter 1). Modern readers must be willing to put themselves, so far as is possible, in the place of John, the visionary in this book, and in the place of his earliest readers. This requires an act of the imagination, for we do not live in John's world—or at least we do not normally think of ourselves as living in John's world. We see ourselves as part of a very different world indeed, with other wonders, and far different threats.

Conservative evangelical students may well protest that these cautions do not apply to them. They believe the Bible to be inspired, and claim not only that John saw what he said he saw, but that his visions reveal to us the way in which our world will end and God's new world will begin. Yet they too need an act of the imagination in order to approach the Book of Revelation with a hope of understanding it. Most of them have not had visions. Most of them have never seen—or at least never recognized—an angel. Their belief in a supernatural world, while quite sincere, is also quite theoretical. They too, in spite of themselves, need a suspension of disbelief to make sense of the Book of Revelation.

Modern students must "become like little children," not only to "enter the kingdom of heaven" (Matt. 18:3) but to enter into the world of John and his visions. This is a difficult thing to do under any circumstances, but it becomes especially difficult when one is at the same time attempting to practice the so-called "historical-critical method."[1] How does a person stand in wonder before a text and try to share something of the spontaneity of the author's experience, while at the same time subjecting the text to careful and dispassionate critical analysis? This is the challenge facing the would-be interpreter of the Book of Revelation.

Two unanswered—perhaps unanswerable—questions complicate the task: First, how spontaneous was the author's visionary experience? Second, how close to the actual experience was the writing? Within the story that unfolds in the Revelation, John is told again and again to write what he has seen (Rev. 1:11, 19; 2:1, 8, 12, 18; 3:1, 7, 14; 14:13; 19:9; 21:5). Once (10:4) he implies that he was writing down everything he saw and heard while it was happening. Yet as he starts to recount his visions, he seems to look back at them from a later perspective, stating that "I was [or came to be] on the island of Patmos" (1:9), just as "I was [or came to be] in the Spirit on the Lord's Day" (1:10). John is not saying necessarily that it is still the Lord's Day as he writes, nor is he still "in the Spirit" in quite the same sense as when he received these visions. Similarly, he is not claiming to write on the island of Patmos.[2] Like all other New Tes-

---

1. See, e.g., in relation to the Synoptic Gospels, Scot McKnight, *Interpreting the Synoptic Gospels* (Grand Rapids: Baker, 1988), Introduction and chaps. 6–8.

2. Isbon T. Beckwith goes so far as to say, "The language implies that he is no longer in Patmos when he wrote this book." *The Apocalypse of John* (Grand Rapids: Baker, 1967 reprint), 434. This is perhaps too strong, but certainly the contrary cannot be assumed.

tament letter writers, John gives his readers' location (1:4, 11) but not his own.[3] A certain distance in time, and perhaps in space, can be assumed between the series of visions described and the writing of the book. The reason this is important is that the visions *in_their literary form* may not be quite so spontaneous as they appear. In narrating his visions the author has adopted certain literary strategies. He has had time to reflect on his experiences and to put them into a form suited to his purposes. Those purposes, of course, can only be determined by careful study of the whole book, paying close attention to both its form and its content.

These considerations may help the student bridge the gap between the need for childlike wonder in reading or hearing the Revelation, as if for the first time, and the need for careful, detailed analysis of its literary structure, its historical and cultural setting, and even the sources of its ideas and language. If the Book of Revelation is based on visions one might expect that its only *source* would be the pure revelation itself. Yet the study of prophetic or millenarian movements reveals that visions and prophecy have never taken place in a vacuum.[4] Invariably their character shapes, and is shaped by, particular historical situations and particular literary and cultural traditions. The sources of prophecies and revelations are both vertical and horizontal: vertical in that they are presumed to come from God, or at least "from above," but horizontal in that they incorporate elements from prophecies and other kinds of literature written decades or centuries before. However immediate or spontaneous such revelations may be, they are inevitably part of one or more continuing traditions and cannot be understood apart from some acquaintance with the traditions to which they belong.

This double character of such a document as the Book of Revelation—transcendent and mysterious, yet anchored in history—means serious students of the work must pay attention to the instruction of Jesus to his disciples to become "as shrewd as snakes and as innocent as doves" (Matt. 10:16). Because the Book of Reve-

---

3. Of the New Testament letters, only 1 Peter reveals its place of origin, and that probably in a symbolic sense ("Babylon," 1 Pet. 5:13).

4. For an excellent example quite far removed from the world of the New Testament, see Hillel Schwartz, *The French Prophets* (Berkeley, Calif.: University of California Press, 1980).

lation is part of history and culture it must be interpreted "from the outside" in light of what can be known of the times in which it was written and the traditions then alive. Yet because it is a self-contained and presumably coherent literary entity, it also must be interpreted "from the inside," in the light of its own internal structure and the signals it sends about the author's purposes. Sometimes both approaches are possible. Sometimes the limits of our historical knowledge allow only the inside view. Nowhere more than in the Book of Revelation will the student be faced with the alternatives of historical or literary interpretation. These two alternatives correspond roughly to the twin questions of what the Book of Revelation is saying and what it is saying it about.

There is no denying that Revelation is a difficult book, but students can take heart from the fact that it was never intended to be a closed book (see 22:10: "Do not seal up the words of the prophecy of this book, for the time is near."). The intention of the author—and the author's God—appears in a parenthetical remark from another New Testament apocalypse: "Let the reader understand" (Mark 13:14).

# Part 1

# General Considerations in the Exegesis of Revelation

# 1

# Genre and Authorship

The first thing many students want to know about a biblical book is who wrote it. But the question of the authorship of the Book of Revelation cannot be separated from another question: "What sort of book is this?" The Guides to New Testament Exegesis series is based on an awareness of, and sensitivity to, the varied literary types or genres comprising the books of the New Testament (see p. 7). Because the author is more likely to be identified in some genres than in others, questions of authorship and genre are intertwined. Nowhere is this more true than in the case of the Book of Revelation. The subject of genre must be addressed with special care in connection with this last book of the New Testament because it seems to represent a *mixed genre* to many readers, sending off mixed signals as to what it intends to be. This is reflected even in the variety of names by which it is known: the "Book of Revelation"; the "Revelation of John"; the "Revelation of Jesus Christ"; the "Apocalypse"; the "Apocalypse of John," or the "Apocalypse of Jesus Christ."

## Apocalypse, Letter, or Prophecy?

Much of the debate over genre concerns whether to translate the Greek word ἀποκάλυψις (*apokalypsis*, 1:1) into English as "revelation" or merely to transliterate it as "apocalypse." Another issue is whether the emphasis should be placed on Jesus Christ as the divine source of the work or on John as the human author. Whatever the name given, the first three verses of the first chapter form the point of departure.

If, however, the next three verses (1:4–6) set the starting point, the result will be quite different, because they bear the unmistakable marks of a New Testament letter, like the letters of Paul. No one refers to the Revelation as the "letter of John," and it would be confusing to do so, because tradition identifies three other short New Testament epistles as John's letters. Yet, ironically the Book of Revelation bears the name of John while 1 John, 2 John, and 3 John do not! A glance at verse 4 shows the same formal characteristics of a letter as all the letters of Paul:

John,
to the seven churches that are in Asia:
Grace and peace from. . . .

Where Paul customarily says, "Grace [mercy] and peace from God our Father and the Lord Jesus Christ," or something similar, this letter has a far more elaborate formula in keeping with the themes and language of the work as a whole: "from the One who is and who was and who is to come, and from the seven spirits that are before his throne, and from Jesus Christ, the faithful witness, the first-born of the dead, and the ruler of the kings of the earth" (vv. 4b–5). And where Paul continues with a blessing or thanksgiving of some kind, this letter continues with a doxology: "To him who loves us and loosed us from our sins in his blood, and made us a kingdom, and priests to his God and Father, to him be glory and power forever and ever. Amen."[1] The letter form is all but forgotten as John proceeds to recount his visions, yet at the end he again takes up the conventions of the Pauline letters with a final benediction: "The grace of the Lord Jesus be with God's people. Amen" (22:21).

If we make "apocalypse" our starting point, we must at the same time acknowledge that the book calls itself an apocalypse once (1:1), but a prophecy or book of prophecy five times (1:3; 22:7, 10, 18–19, and possibly 19:10). This raises the question of whether a distinction is intended between "apocalypse" and "prophecy," or whether the latter, in the author's mind, interprets the former. The continuity

---

1. Compare Gal. 1:5, a rare instance in which Paul does not have a blessing or thanksgiving: "to whom be glory forever and ever. Amen."

between "apocalypse" in 1:1 and "prophecy" in 1:3 suggests that the terms are almost interchangeable. Paul includes both "apocalypse" and "prophecy" in 1 Corinthians 14:6 (along with "knowledge" and "teaching") in a list of different kinds of utterances by prophets in the congregation (see also vv. 26–33: "psalm," "teaching," "apocalypse," "tongue," "interpretation"). In such instances the Greek word ἀποκάλυψις (*apokalypsis*) or *apocalypse* should be translated, not merely transliterated, into English as "revelation," on the assumption that a revelation is an oracle of some kind granted to a Christian prophet. Similarly, the Book of Revelation seems to present itself as a long oracle of one such prophet, not unlike the prophetic books of the Hebrew Bible.[2] *Apocalypse* is here interpreted to mean simply "a prophecy," not in the narrow sense of a prediction of the future—although the Book of Revelation surely claims to be that—but in the broader sense of a direct revelation from God about past, present, or future events, to an individual or group qualified to disclose the revelation to a larger community of believers.

## Apocalyptic Literature

The "Apocalypse" has also given its name to a large body of Jewish and Christian literature outside as well as within the Hebrew and Christian Bibles. Even beginning students become familiar with the umbrella term *Jewish apocalyptic literature*, comprising the biblical book of Daniel and a number of early Jewish works bearing the names of well known or less familiar characters from the Hebrew Bible. These include collected cycles of tradition about Enoch, "in the seventh generation from Adam" (see Jude 14), who "walked with God; and he was not, for God took him" (Gen. 5:24). Stories about Enoch's heavenly visions were collected in the apocalypses known as *1 Enoch* (now fully extant only in Ethiopic manuscripts) and *2*

---

2. On prophecy as a religious and social phenomenon in early Christianity, the student should consult David E. Aune, *Prophecy in Early Christianity and the Ancient Mediterranean World* (Grand Rapids: Eerdmans, 1983) and the primary and secondary literature Aune cites. A far less comprehensive, but more theological treatment, is that of David Hill, *New Testament Prophecy* (London: Marshall, Morgan, and Scott, 1979).

*Enoch* (known largely from Old Slavonic texts). Many of Enoch's visions centered on the evil union between fallen angels and human beings hinted at in Genesis 6:1–4, and on God's consequent punishment of both angels and humans at the time of the flood.

Other Jewish apocalypses dealt with God's judgment on Israel and Jerusalem in the time of the exile. These include the Latin *4 Ezra* (sometimes called *2 Esdras*), attributed to Ezra the scribe, which found its way into the Old Testament Apocrypha. Two others not included in the Apocrypha, the Syriac *2 Baruch* and Greek *3 Baruch*, were attributed to Jeremiah's scribe with that name. The apocalypses of Ezra and Baruch all come from a time shortly *after* the Book of Revelation and share with Revelation a strong interest in the fate of Jerusalem. *Fourth Ezra*, with its visions of Jerusalem, and *1 Enoch*, with its journeys to heaven, are probably the most relevant apocalypses for the student of the Revelation.

Other Jewish apocalypses attributed to major figures in Jewish tradition are the *Testament* (or Assumption) *of Moses*, the *Apocalypse of Abraham*, the *Apocalypse of Adam*, and the *Apocalypse of Elijah*. These and many more Jewish apocalyptic writings are available to students in a recent comprehensive collection in English translation.[3] Apocalyptic features can also be found in earlier Jewish works that are not themselves considered apocalyptic: passages in Isaiah and Ezekiel, such writings of early Judaism as *Jubilees* and the *Testaments of the Twelve Patriarchs*, the Dead Sea Scrolls,[4] and passages in the New Testament itself.[5]

---

3. James H. Charlesworth, ed., *The Old Testament Pseudepigrapha*, Vol. 1 (Garden City, N.Y.: Doubleday, 1983). A less complete collection is H. F. D. Sparks, ed., *The Apocryphal Old Testament* (Oxford: Clarendon, 1984). An older collection, R. H. Charles, ed., *The Apocrypha and Pseudepigrapha of the Old Testament, Vol. 2* (Oxford: Clarendon, 1913) is still of considerable value because of its detailed, if sometimes outdated, introductions. A convenient brief anthology for the student who wants to sample the flavor of this literature is M. G. Reddish, ed., *Apocalyptic Literature: A Reader* (Nashville: Abingdon, 1990), esp. chaps. 1–2.

4. For Jubilees and the Testaments of the Twelve Patriarchs, see Charlesworth, *Pseudepigrapha* (Jubilees is in vol. 2); for the Dead Sea Scrolls (Qumran literature) see Geza Vermes, *The Dead Sea Scrolls in English* (New York: Penguin, 1987), and Reddish, *Apocalyptic*, 224–40.

5. In the New Testament see, for example, Mark 13; 1 Thess. 4:13–18; 2 Thess. 2:1–12; 1 Cor. 15:20–26, 51–53.

In ancient Christianity, the term *apocalypse* eventually was applied to a number of works recounting visions. These were ascribed to famous Christian apostles (for example, the *Apocalypse of Peter*, the *Apocalypse of Paul*) or Old Testament figures (for example, the *Ascension of Isaiah*).[6] The designation of these works as apocalypses is probably attributable to the tendency of popular noncanonical (apocryphal) Christian writings to duplicate the genres represented in the canon of the New Testament. There are apocryphal gospels (for example, of Thomas, Peter, and Philip), apocryphal Acts (for example, of Thomas, Peter, Paul, and John), apocryphal letters (allegedly from the Apostles or from Paul to the Corinthians and the Laodiceans). It is not surprising, therefore, that there should be apocryphal apocalypses as well. Another early Christian practice was to subject Jewish apocalyptic writings to Christian interpolation and revision to give them a Christian slant and claim them for the church. Brief Christian apocalypses were even prefixed or appended to Jewish apocalypses for the same purpose. The best examples of the latter procedure are chapters 1–2 and 15–16 of *4 Ezra*, sometimes known as *5 Ezra* and *6 Ezra*, respectively.

Apocalyptic literature, Jewish or Christian, is a field of study with which the student of Revelation must gain familiarity.[7] Yet limits must be drawn, or the student will be swallowed up in the sea of apocalyptic literature and never get to the text of Revelation itself. The matter is complicated by the fact that the study of apocalyptic literature has undergone significant changes in the past two decades, and many questions remain. The crucial question is whether *apocalypse* is properly called a genre, or whether it is simply a mood or temperament—or perhaps a religious perspective or

---

6. The best collections of these ancient Christian works are E. Hennecke and W. Schneemelcher, eds., *New Testament Apocrypha*, Vol. 2 (London: Lutterworth, 1965), and M. R. James, ed., *The Apocryphal New Testament* (Oxford: Clarendon, 1924). See also Reddish, *Apocalyptic*, chaps. 4–6.

7. See, for example, D. S. Russell, *The Method and Message of Jewish Apocalyptic, 200 B.C. to A.D. 100* (Philadelphia: Westminster, 1964); Klaus Koch, *The Rediscovery of Apocalyptic* (London: SCM, 1972); Paul D. Hanson, *The Dawn of Apocalyptic*, rev. ed. (Philadelphia: Fortress, 1979); idem, *Old Testament Apocalyptic* (Nashville: Abingdon, 1987); Christopher Rowland, *The Open Heaven: A Study of Apocalyptic in Judaism and Early Christianity* (New York: Crossroad, 1982), and John J. Collins, *The Apocalyptic Imagination* (New York: Crossroad, 1984).

theology—that expresses itself in a variety of forms and genres. Is the Book of Revelation an apocalypse or is it simply "apocalyptic" in its view of God and the world, and in the imagery it employs? Recent attempts have been made to define *apocalypse*. A widely used definition is that proposed by the Apocalypse Seminar of the Society of Biblical Literature in 1979: "*Apocalypse* is a genre of revelatory literature with a narrative framework, in which a revelation is mediated by an otherworldly being to a human recipient, disclosing a transcendent reality which is both temporal, insofar as it envisages eschatological salvation, and spatial, insofar as it involves another, supernatural world."[8]

In 1986 the definition was enlarged by adding that the genre called *apocalypse* was "intended to interpret present earthly circumstances in light of the supernatural world and of the future, and to influence both the understanding and the behavior of the audience by means of divine authority."[9]

The beginning student, staggering under such verbosity, will do well to remember that definitions of this kind are almost inevitably circular. Scholars assemble a group of documents suspected of belonging to a genre called *apocalypse* and list the common features of these documents to define the genre. For example, the definition quoted above appears to be tailored to fit the Book of Revelation, or at least to make sure of its inclusion. This seems natural since Revelation is the first known work in Greek to title itself "apocalypse."

It would be very easy to assemble a group of Jewish and early Christian writings which had one other common feature: authorship attributed to a great or wise man either of the distant Jewish

---

8. This definition is found in the article by John J. Collins, "Introduction: Towards the Morphology of a Genre," *Semeia* 14 (1979): 9. The whole of vol. 14 of this journal was devoted to apocalypse as a genre. An even more extensive collection of essays is David Hellholm, ed., *Apocalypticism in the Mediterranean World and the Near East* (Tübingen: J. C. B. Mohr [Paul Siebeck], 1983).

9. For this amendment, see Adela Yarbro Collins, "Introduction: Early Christian Apocalypticism," *Semeia* 36 (1986): 7. While *Semeia* 14 looked at apocalyptic literature in general, vol. 36 focused on proposed early Christian examples of the apocalyptic genre. Both volumes are important for the serious student. For a good introductory discussion that takes account of this recent research, see David E. Aune, *The New Testament in its Literary Environment* (Philadelphia: Westminster, 1987), 226–52.

past (Enoch, Ezra, or Baruch) or of the more recent Christian past (Peter or Paul). This literary device is known as *pseudonymity* (assigning a false name), and writings that employ this device are traditionally labeled *pseudepigrapha* (false writings), a term reflecting the Christian church's negative judgment on their legitimacy and worth. The latter include, but are not limited to, documents of an apocalyptic kind.[10] A collection of such apocalypses would *not* include the Book of Revelation, nor would it include one other early Christian writing almost equally conspicuous for its apocalyptic features, the so-called *Shepherd of Hermas*.[11] Neither John, who speaks in the Book of Revelation, nor Hermas, who recounts his visions in the *Shepherd of Hermas*, is identifiable as a great man of the Jewish or Christian past. No certain knowledge of either exists apart from the works that bear their name.

## Who Was John?

Attempts have been made to identify the "John" of Revelation 1:1, 4, 9, and 22:8 with some other John mentioned in the New Testament or early church tradition. Josephine Massyngberde Ford identified him as John the Baptist,[12] but it would be difficult to find even one other scholar who shares that opinion. An ancient tradition going back to Justin Martyr and Irenaeus in the second century identified him as the apostle John, son of Zebedee, who with his brother James and two others left his fishing net to follow Jesus at the beginning of Jesus' public ministry (Mark 1:19–20). The tradition commonly assumed that this John was the "beloved disciple" who leaned on Jesus' breast at the last supper, and to whom the

---

10. Notice that the "pseudepigrapha" included in the collections both of Charlesworth (*Pseudepigrapha*) and of Charles (*Apocrypha and Pseudepigrapha*) include other than apocalyptic works (see esp. vol. 2 of Charlesworth).

11. The *Shepherd of Hermas* is ordinarily counted among the second-century writings known as the apostolic fathers. For the text, see *The Apostolic Fathers*, Loeb Classical Library (London: William Heinemann, 1913), 2.1–305; also G. F. Snyder in *The Apostolic Fathers: A New Translation and Commentary, Vol. 6* (Camden, N.J.: Thomas Nelson, 1968), and J. B. Lightfoot and J. R. Harmer, *The Apostolic Fathers*, 2d ed., rev. and ed. Michael W. Holmes (Grand Rapids: Baker, 1989), 189–290.

12. *Revelation*. Anchor Bible 38 (Garden City, N.Y.: Doubleday, 1975), 28.

authorship of the fourth Gospel is attributed (John 21:20–24).[13] Other ancient theories identified him with the "John Mark" mentioned in Acts 12:12 (also 12:25; 13:5, 13; 15:37, 39),[14] or with a certain "John the Elder," said to have been confused later in Ephesus with John the son of Zebedee.[15]

All these theories attempted to identify the author of Revelation "from the outside." This is one way to approach not only the matter of authorship, but many other questions raised by this book. In the case of authorship, it entails a considerable amount of guesswork. Still, this path is taken by those with a high degree of respect for church tradition. Ironically, this group includes many evangelicals who have been taught to base their conclusions, *not* on tradition, but solely on the biblical text. Those who follow the latter approach consistently will try to answer all questions, so far as is possible, "from the inside," that is, entirely from data supplied by the text of Revelation.

In the case of authorship, this means being content with the information that the author's name is John. Clearly, John does not feel the need for self-introduction in his greeting (1:4),[16] adding only a brief self-description in 1:9 as "your brother and companion in the persecution and kingdom and patient endurance that are ours in Jesus." Because his intended audience knows him, the modern reader learns little about him. He is a "servant" of Jesus Christ (1:1b), and as such is part of a group called "servants" (1:1a) of Jesus

---

13. For the evidence, see the major commentaries; also Daniel J. Theron, *Evidence of Tradition* (Grand Rapids: Baker, 1957), 25–33, 89–91, 107–13. This is the basis for the common assumption today among conservative Christians that the Gospel of John, the three Epistles of John, and the Revelation of John are all the work of the apostle John, the son of Zebedee.

14. Dionysius, Bishop of Alexandria, is said to have entertained this possibility in the third century, but he rejected it. See Eusebius *Ecclesiastical History* 7.25.15 (Loeb Classical Library, 2.203). The whole discussion which Eusebius cites from Dionysius (7.25) is of great interest even today for students of the Book of Revelation.

15. See Eusebius *Ecclesiastical History* 3.39.5–7 (Loeb Classical Library, 1.293). This tradition found support in the second-century report of Papias, a Bishop in Asia Minor, and perhaps also in the designation, "the Elder," for the author of 2 John and 3 John. It was also the preferred solution of Dionysius (7.25.16), and for a time found wide acceptance among modern scholars. See most recently Martin Hengel, *The Johannine Question* (Philadelphia: Trinity, 1989).

16. Compare Paul in 1 and 2 Thessalonians. In his other letters, Paul always adds a self-designation such as "servant of God," or "apostle of Jesus Christ."

or God. An angel closely associates him with his "brothers the prophets" (22:9) or his "brothers who have the testimony of Jesus" (19:10). Jesus addresses him with a plural pronoun, apparently as part of this larger group: "I, Jesus, sent my angel to testify these things to you [plural] about the churches" (22:16a).[17]

It is fair to conclude from this inside evidence that the author writes as an early Christian prophet to a group of churches that knew and respected his prophetic authority. Whatever else John may have been—apostle, elder, evangelist, baptizer—is not discovered in the text. Although he knows of "the Twelve Apostles of the Lamb," and sees their names inscribed on the foundations of the new Jerusalem (21:14), he gives no hint of belonging to their number. He makes no claim to apostolic authority; if he is an apostle he conceals the fact.

## Genre: Toward a Conclusion

A pseudonymous apocalypse of John based on traditions about the apostle John, the son of Zebedee, would probably have capitalized on the account in the fourth Gospel of the beloved disciple reclining on Jesus' breast (John 13:23) and would have recorded the secret revelations this disciple received in his position of privilege and intimacy. Obviously, Revelation is not that kind of an apocalypse. Instead, like the *Shepherd of Hermas*, it is based on a series of visions otherwise unknown, seen by someone writing in his own name. It does not capitalize on an old story, but tells a new one. Although the Revelation fits some definitions of an apocalypse, the author's self-references suggest that he wrote as a Christian prophet. His work stands as evidence that Christian prophecy very early took on features that previously had been more characteristic of Jewish apocalypses than of biblical prophecy: visions or revelations "mediated by an otherworldly being," and "disclosing a transcendent reality" both of "eschatological salvation" and a "supernatural world" (see footnote 8).

---

17. On this verse, see David E. Aune, "The Prophetic Circle of the John of Patmos and the Exegesis of Revelation 22.16," *Journal for the Study of the New Testament* 37 (1989): 103–16.

Yet it must not be forgotten that this particular prophecy has been put into the form of a letter. To speak of mixed genres is to admit the limitations—even, perhaps, the futility—of genre classification. The simplest solution to the problem of the Revelation's genre is to consider it a letter. There is no doubt (as with apocalypses) that such a genre existed in antiquity. We see from the letters of Paul and others the formal characteristics of early Christian letters much better than we understand the characteristics of early Christian prophecies. Neither Romans nor 1 Corinthians, but Revelation, is the longest letter in the New Testament.

This long letter from John is not a personal letter, as is 3 John or Philemon, nor is it written to a single congregation as are most of Paul's. It is a general or catholic letter as are 1 Peter, 2 Peter, Jude, and James, a type represented among Paul's letters by Galatians (to the churches of Galatia in Asia Minor) and possibly Ephesians.[18] Instead of being shared by two congregations at most, like Colossians (Col. 4:16), Revelation is a circular letter intended to pass through seven congregations in Asia Minor.[19]

A conspicuous feature of the author's style is the use of first-person narrative. Although writing in first-person style is compatible with the modes of prophetic or apocalyptic literature,[20] it most resembles the style of a letter. Unlike the anonymous and largely impersonal Gospels and Acts,[21] the letters of the New Testament are communications in which a self-conscious "I" personally addresses a singular or plural "you." It is no accident that Paul is the most mem-

---

18. Ephesians is a general letter if the words "in Ephesus" are omitted in 1:1b (as in a number of important ancient manuscripts, followed by the RSV). Otherwise, it presents itself as a letter to the Christian congregation at Ephesus.

19. See also 1 Peter, written as a circular letter for an unspecified number of Asian congregations spread over a much larger area (1 Pet. 1:1), and notice also that the congregation with which the letter to the Colossians is to be shared (Laodicea) is one of the seven congregations addressed in the Book of Revelation.

20. Aune, in attempting to define the apocalyptic genre "with special reference to the Apocalypse of John," significantly makes this "autobiographical form" part of his definition. See his article, "The Apocalypse of John and the Problem of Genre," *Semeia* 36 (1986): 86–87.

21. Only very rarely in the Gospels and Acts does the writer (or a source) allow the reader even a glimpse of his or her personality (for example, "I" in Luke 1:3–4 and John 21:25; "we" in John 1:14, and in the so-called "we" passages of Acts: 16:11–17; 20:5–15; 21:1–18; 27:1–28:16).

orable "personality" in the New Testament for he wrote the most letters! The John of Revelation is not a personality in quite the same sense as Paul, but he too, by his visionary experiences, shares something of himself with his readers. Unlike Paul, who shared his visions only with reticence, sometimes even avoiding first-person narration (2 Cor. 12:1–4), John does not hesitate to go into great detail about what he has seen and heard "in the Spirit" (Rev. 1:10). He invites his readers unabashedly into his experiences, so that they may see what he saw, hear what he heard, and understand its significance.

John's long letter contains a narrative, a story line. The story is apocalyptic in detailing visions mediated by angelic figures and prophetic in exhorting the churches with words of warning and encouragement. The closest Paul comes in his letters to such a narrative is his autobiographical testimony in Galatians 1:11–2:14. If a more specific genre than letter or circular letter is needed, the Revelation should be classified as either a *prophetic letter* on the basis of the long title prefixed to the letter proper (1:1–3) or an *apocalyptic letter* because of its content.[22]

The discussion of Revelation's genre demonstrates how "stretched" the scholars' generic categories can become when they begin to deal with real literature, particularly good literature. Many literary theorists have suggested that good, and especially great, works never quite belong to a single genre. They are highly individual creations that expand the categories to the breaking point.[23] This is certainly true of the Book of Revelation. If a letter, it is like no

---

22. A good example of an apocalyptic letter is 2 Baruch 78–87 (see Charlesworth, *Pseudepigrapha*, 1.78–87). However, it has more striking similarities to 1 Peter than to Revelation, differing from the latter especially in that it is not the record of a vision. See J. Ramsey Michaels, "Jewish and Christian Apocalyptic Letters: 1 Peter, Revelation, and 2 Baruch 78–87," in 1987 Society of Biblical Literature Seminar Papers (1987): 268–75.

23. This is acknowledged by more than one school of literary criticism. See Adrian Marino, "Toward a Definition of Literary Genres," in Joseph P. Strelka, ed., *Theories of Literary Genre*, Yearbook of Comparative Literature 8 (University Park, Penn.: Pennsylvania State University Press, 1978), 51; Adena Rosmarin, *The Power of Genre* (Minneapolis: University of Minnesota Press, 1985), 45; Jacques Derrida, "The Law of Genre," *Critical Inquiry* 7 (1980): 63–66; E. D. Hirsch, *Validity in Interpretation* (New Haven: Yale University Press, 1967). Among biblical scholars see Edgar V. McKnight, *Postmodern Use of the Bible: The Emergence of Reader-oriented Criticism* (Nashville: Abingdon, 1988), 242–44.

other early Christian letter we possess. If an apocalypse, it is like no other apocalypse. If a prophecy, it is unique among prophecies.

Those who bring to the book a set of expectations based on a particular genre can expect to be surprised sooner or later—probably sooner. For example, when we start with the quite reasonable notion that Revelation is a letter, we quickly discover that the letter form is little more than a framework. His visions so captivate John that through most of the book he forgets his role as letter writer! There is room to be skeptical about how crucial the determination of genre is for the interpretation of specific passages. Despite frequent claims that an understanding of genre determines interpretation, is it really true that a person will interpret, for example, Revelation 7:9–17; 12:1–6, or 20:1–10 differently, depending on whether the book is judged to be a prophecy, an apocalypse, or a letter? Students in a course on Revelation might try a test case, attempting to interpret a given text, first as if it were part of an early Christian letter, second as a section of an apocalypse, and third as a piece of prophecy. Does the meaning come out differently or the same?

One further caution: while genres are normally assigned to whole literary works, the student of the Revelation needs to be as sensitive to the parts as to the whole. The student will most likely work on a specific passage, rather than the whole book. This is certainly the case if the goal is sermon preparation. For example, if the whole book is a letter, it is hardly plausible to refer (as is common) to the communications in chapters 2–3 as the "seven letters" or "letters to the seven churches." To speak of letters within a letter does not make sense, and there is no textual evidence that these messages were ever separated so that each congregation received only the communication bearing its name. The blessing on the reader in Revelation 1:3 implies that the entire book was read publicly in every church, allowing each to hear the reading of each other's mail (chaps. 1–3)—and a great deal more (chaps. 4–22).

If the communications in chapters 2–3 are not letters, what are they? They have a common form and structure and appear to be prophetic oracles (like the oracles against the nations in Amos 1–2). It recently has been suggested that these oracles have been put into the form of royal or imperial edicts in order to contrast the sovereign decrees of Christ the King with those of the Roman emperor.[24] Prophetic oracles in the Hebrew Bible were often preceded or accompanied by narratives of the prophet's call (for example, Isa. 6:1–13; Jer. 1:4–19, and Ezek. 2:1–3:15), and this is the case with Revelation 2–3 (see 1:9–20). There is yet another "call narrative" (10:1–11), which is followed by more visions and oracles (see 10:11: "You must prophesy again"). There are accounts of being taken up to heaven (4:1–6), abrupt glimpses into the heavenly temple (11:19; 15:5–8), various visions of heaven and earth accompanied on occasion by explanations of certain details in the visions (for example, chaps. 7, 12–14, 17), and at least one extended oracle describing verbally to John what will happen (11:1–13).

In short, one must be prepared for variety in attempting to read and interpret the Book of Revelation. The judgment that it is a letter, an apocalypse, or a prophecy will not necessarily take the student very far. The form of a specific passage under discussion is at least as important to the interpretive task as the genre of the entire book.

---

24. See David E. Aune, "The Form and Function of the Proclamations to the Seven Churches (Revelation 2–3)," *New Testament Studies* 36.2 (1990): 182–204.

# 2

# Historical and Social Setting

The Book of Revelation is a work filled with visions and the supernatural. If it were written today it would be called a work of the imagination. Yet it is natural to assume, with most interpreters, that the visionary world of this book intersected the real world of the author and his readers. As with the Gospels and Pauline Epistles, it is imperative to learn as much as possible about the historical, social, and political situation from which Revelation emerged and to which it spoke.

## The Seven Churches in Their Local Setting

Much background information is available on the oracles or messages to the seven churches of Asia Minor in chapters 2–3: Ephesus, Smyrna, Pergamum, Thyatira, Sardis, Philadelphia, and Laodicea. These were cities and congregations in the late first and early second century. Paul's activities in Ephesus are described in Acts 19–20. He wrote a letter to Colosse near Laodicea (Col. 2:1; 4:13, 15) and instructed that his letter also be read to the Laodiceans (4:16). He wrote a letter to Philemon and Apphia in a house church in the same vicinity, and perhaps one to Ephesus as well (see p. 30, f.n. 18). Ignatius, Bishop of Antioch, wrote letters in the early second century to Ephesus, Smyrna, and Philadelphia as well as Tralles and Magnesia. One of Smyrna's bishops was Polycarp, and Melito, another early Christian writer, was bishop of Sardis.

Clearly these were not all the Christian congregations in Asia Minor. Besides Tralles and Magnesia there was Hierapolis, to which Paul refers (Col. 4:13) and whose bishop in the middle of the second century is known to have been named Papias.[1] Quite possibly John's choice of seven out of all the congregations that existed in Asia Minor at the time he wrote was a literary device related to his symbolic use of the number seven throughout his book.[2] Yet few would argue that the churches themselves are a literary device. Rather, they are the closest link we have between the visions of Revelation and historical reality. Therefore, those who insist that the Revelation is not mere imagination but actual history tend to make these churches, and the prophetic oracles of chapters 2 and 3, their starting point.

William M. Ramsay's classic 1909 work surveyed the historical, geographical, and archaeological data on the seven churches available to scholars at the turn of the twentieth century.[3] Ramsay argued that these seven churches were chosen, and in this order, because they represented an established postal route for a letter to the Asian mainland, with Ephesus the natural point of entry.[4] He claimed each of the seven churches represented a district (for example, Laodicea could represent its neighbors Colosse and Hierapolis). This theory was based on the assumption that John was still on the island of Patmos when he wrote the letter, an assumption that is possible but not quite certain (see pp. 16–17).

---

1. Eusebius *Ecclesiastical History* 3.36.2.

2. The Muratorian Canon, probably in the late 2d century, argued that John chose to write to seven churches as a way of addressing the whole church throughout the world, and found in this a parallel with the seven churches to which Paul wrote letters. See Daniel J. Theron, *Evidence of Tradition* (Grand Rapids: Baker, 1957), 111.

3. *The Letters to the Seven Churches of Asia and Their Place in the Plan of the Apocalypse* (London: Hodder and Stoughton). Students who use this standard source are often unaware of the extensive work with inscriptions and other primary sources on which it is based. See, for example, *The Historical Geography of Asia Minor*, Royal Geographical Society Supplementary Papers 4 (London: John Murray, 1890), and *The Cities and Bishoprics of Phrygia*, Vol. 1 (Oxford: Clarendon, 1895).

4. Ramsay, *Letters*, 185–96. Ramsay argued for this in more detail in his article, "Roads and Travel in New Testament Times," in James Hastings, ed., *Dictionary of the Bible*, Vol. 5 (Edinburgh: T. and T. Clark, 1904), 375–402. He also appealed to a similar suggestion by F. J. A. Hort regarding 1 Peter (*The First Epistle of St. Peter, I.1–II.17* (London: Macmillan, 1898), 157–84.

Despite his credentials as a great historian, Ramsay's concerns in this book were as much apologetic as historical. His historical research had led him to the firm conviction that the Bible referred to actual places and events and that its testimony about those places was accurate. This conviction found confirmation for him in the historical realism of the so-called "seven letters." At times his search for realism leads him to confuse the congregations addressed with their cities. He explains certain details in the messages to the churches by referring to aspects of the city's reputation in the Roman empire, or to incidents in the city's history. For example, he explains Christ's warning to Sardis ("If you do not awake, I will come as a thief, and you will not know in what hour I will come upon you," 3:3) not simply in relation to the Gospel tradition (Matt. 24:42–44; Luke 12:39–40), but with reference to two incidents in Sardis' history in which the city was caught unprepared by hostile armies.[5] To Ramsay this is not a confusion but a consciously held perspective on what a church is:

> The Church of Sardis is not merely in the city of Sardis, it is in a sense the city; and the Christians are the people of the city. There is not in his mind the slightest idea that Christians are to keep out of the world—as might, perhaps, be suggested from an overly exclusive contemplation of some parts of the Revelation; the Church is here addressed, apparently with the set purpose of suggesting that the fortunes of ancient Sardis had been its own fortunes, that it had endured those sieges, committed those faults of carelessness and blind confidence, and sunk into the same decay and death as the city.[6]

Ramsay's is an intriguing interpretation of the New Testament understanding of the church. It has had no discernible impact, however, on subsequent discussions of Revelation from a sociological standpoint, and Ramsay himself seemed to recognize that it ran counter to the conflict between church and world which so dominates many of John's visions. Yet this view of the church influences his discussion of every one of the seven churches. He describes Smyrna as a "faithful" city (to Rome)[7] and finds in this a key to the

5. Ramsay, *Letters*, 377–78.
6. Ibid., 380.
7. Ibid., 254.

exhortation to the congregation at Smyrna to "be faithful even to death, and I will give you the crown of life" (Rev. 2:10).[8] Ephesus was considered a "city of change" because of the silting up of its harbor over centuries,[9] and the church at Ephesus is threatened with change, the removal of its lampstand.[10] Philadelphia was a "missionary city" in that it was intended to be a center for the spread of Hellenism through Asia Minor,[11] and the church at Philadelphia is given an "open door" for missionary activity in the spread of Christianity.[12] Ramsay called Laodicea a "city of compromise," a center of trade and finance, able to "adapt itself to the needs and wishes of others, ever pliable and accommodating," and the congregation at Laodicea was much the same, "neither hot nor cold," but lukewarm.[13]

One has the feeling that Ramsay's summary of each city's history is shaped by what he already knows of the prophetic message directed to each congregation. His parallels between the cities and the churches are often more impressive as sermon illustrations than as solid interpretive tools. While profiting immensely from the historical data that this classic work provides, students should be aware that few would read Paul's letters in this way, and that consequently they should be cautious about applying such a method to this apocalyptic letter of John.

The scholarly tradition of Ramsay is maintained and, more important, updated and corrected in the work of Colin J. Hemer.[14] Hemer offers a cautious critique of his predecessor,[15] but argues that "there is at times some measure of identification of church with city." He admits that "this idea needs cautious handling, but we must recognize the remarkable strength and individuality of environmental influence in ancient city life. The churches are apt

---

8. Ibid., 275.

9. Ibid., 233.

10. Ibid., 243.

11. Ibid., 391–92.

12. Ibid., 405.

13. Ibid., 423–24.

14. *The Letters to the Seven Churches of Asia in Their Local Setting*, Journal for the Study of the New Testament Supplement Series 11 (Sheffield, England: JSOT, 1986). For a brief, factual handbook on these cities, see also Edwin M. Yamauchi, *New Testament Cities in Western Asia Minor* (Grand Rapids: Baker, 1980).

15. Hemer, *Letters*, 25–26.

to be judged by their varying response to their surroundings."[16] His comment suggests that Ramsay's approach may be more valid in connection with churches that have conformed to their pagan environment (Sardis and Laodicea), than with those that stood firm against the social pressures of the city and the empire (Smyrna and Philadephia). While there may be an identification of sorts between the churches and the cities, it is never desirable to the author of Revelation; on the contrary it is precisely what he hates and fears most.

Hemer leaves it to others to develop the sociological perspective of John and his community. His interest is in history, not sociology, and he is more self-conscious than is Ramsay about his methodology and use of sources.[17] Given this, and the fact that his work is much more recent, Hemer is the more helpful guide to students on the historical circumstances of the seven cities and their churches. Hemer hesitates to contradict Ramsay, even when his own evidence and observations seem to demand it. Yet his insistence that one should look first to the Old Testament as the source of John's imagery, and only then to local references about the cities of Asia,[18] serves as a corrective to Ramsay's approach.[19] A greater sensitivity to John's use of the sayings of Jesus (whether oral or written) might have helped even more.[20]

Another strength of Hemer's contribution is his recognition that the messages to the seven churches must not be isolated from the Book of Revelation as a whole.[21] He demonstrates three ways in which chapters 2–3 are linked to the rest of the book: (1) parallels

---

16. Ibid., 21.

17. Ibid., 20–21.

18. Ibid., 20, 210.

19. The possibility of "local references" in the seven messages is obviously legitimate, despite its exaggeration by Ramsay (and to some extent by Hemer). The best concise summary of such possible references (in the context of a perceptive critique of Ramsay) is that of John M. Court, *Myth and History in the Book of Revelation* (Atlanta: John Knox, 1979), 20–42.

20. See, for example, Ramsay's interpretation, which Hemer endorses, of Rev. 3:2–3 in light of the history of Sardis, rather than of Jesus' image of the thief (esp. Matt. 24:36–25:13) and his repeated exhortations to "watch" or "stay awake." Paul's use of this material in 1 Thess. 5:1–11 suggests that local history is not needed to explain John's (actually Jesus') language.

21. Hemer, *Letters*, 14, 16.

between Christ's self-description at the beginning of each of the seven messages and John's initial vision of Christ in the first chapter;[22] (2) parallels between promises given in the seven messages and the visions of triumph in chapters 19–22;[23] (3) parallels between the seven messages and the rest of the visions of the book. The first link is definite and clear-cut, the second only slightly less so, but in the case of the third Hemer comments, with good reason, "Here the parallels lend themselves even less to analysis. . . . A few of the correspondences are close and illuminating, but in general the reminiscences are elusive and marginal."[24]

If one feature of Revelation poses a problem for readers today, it is this difficulty in linking up chapters 2–3 with the rest of the book. It is no accident that most ministers who preach from the Revelation at all tend to confine themselves to the first three chapters. Chapters 2–3 seem to address situations not too far removed from those facing many American churches today. These churches are not being persecuted. Only two (Smyrna and Philadelphia) are warned of future persecution, while one (Pergamum) is reminded of past persecution. The fact that one past martyr can be singled out (Antipas in Pergamum, 2:13) suggests that martyrdom is by no means a familiar experience. These churches are outwardly at peace, although Smyrna and Philadelphia face slander from Jews or Judaizing Gentiles (2:9 and 3:9), and Ephesus, Pergamum, and Thyatira are, or have been, divided into factions over the teachings of would-be prophets or apostles.[25] Their most serious problem is complacency, a danger everywhere, but particularly at Ephesus, Sardis, and Laodicea. Ephesus has lost its "first love" (2:4); Sardis is "dead" (3:1), and Laodicea is "neither hot nor cold" (3:16). When the risen Christ threatens the churches, it is not with persecution at

22. Compare 2:1 with 1:13, 16; 2:8 with 1:17–18; 2:12 with 1:16; 2:18 with 1:14–15; 3:1 with 1:4, 16; 3:7 with 1:18 (cf. 6:10), and 3:14 with 1:5 (cf. 19:11).

23. Compare 2:7 with 22:2, 14, 19; 2:11 with 20:6, 14, and 21:8; 2:17 with 19:12; 2:26–27 with 19:15 (cf. 12:5); 3:5 with 20:12, 15 and 21:27 (cf. 13:8, 17:8); 3:12 with 21:2, 10 (cf. 19:12), and 3:21 with 20:4.

24. Hemer, *Letters*, 16.

25. Ephesus has solved its problem with false apostles (2:2), and with the so-called "Nicolaitans" (2:6). Pergamum (2:14–15) and Thyatira (2:20–23) still struggle with the latter, who are probably the group being described under the biblical names of Balaam (2:14) and Jezebel (2:20).

the hands of the Romans, but with divine judgment at his own coming.[26]

No preacher who has tried to continue a series of sermons beyond chapters 2 and 3 needs to be told that chapters 4–19 are very different indeed. The whole world is troubled, and Christian believers now find themselves in "great tribulation" (Rev. 7:14) at the hands of human enemies and human institutions. The believers that John sees in these visions are consistently faithful to their confession.[27] There are no factions, no false teaching, no complacency. Most of them—perhaps all—are put to death "for the word of God and for the testimony which they had" (6:9; 20:4). Yet in the end God vindicates them and destroys their enemies, with blood flowing as high as the horses' bridles (14:20; 19:15–21). The dead believers will come to life, reign with Christ for a thousand years, and serve him forever in a new Jerusalem.

It must be recognized that the future portrayed in Revelation 4–22 is not a future held out indiscriminately to everyone in the seven churches. It is a future awaiting the congregations at Smyrna and Philadelphia, and those in the other churches who listen to John's warnings and "overcome" the factions and the complacency now threatening them. Those whom John opposes, and those who ignore his warnings, will not face persecution because they will be on the side of the persecutors and will share their fate. The great conflict between good and evil documented in Revelation, therefore, is more than a conflict *between* the seven Asian congregations and the Roman Empire. It is also a conflict *within* most of the congregations. In teaching the Book of Revelation I have occasionally asked students to assume the role of reader or hearer in one of those seven congregations. They must try to imagine how they might have reacted to whatever passage from chapters 4–22 is under discussion and how the passage might have been understood in that setting. Although this is a work of imagination rather than critical research, it is a way of keeping the seven churches in view and of doing justice to the fact that the whole

---

26. See, for example, 2:5, 16, 22–23; 3:3. John also holds out hope in relation to Christ's coming (2:25; 3:11, 20).

27. Occasionally a voice like that heard in chaps. 2–3 breaks in to urge readers to see to it that this is the case, such as the call for wisdom in 13:18, for patience in 14:12, and for spiritual wakefulness in 16:15.

book—not just the seven messages—was written to be read aloud to each of the seven congregations.

## Liars: A Case Study

The fundamental unity between the seven messages of chapters 2–3 and the visions of chapters 4–22 can be illustrated from a brief word study of *liars* and *lying*. John commends the church at Ephesus because "you have tested those who claim to be apostles, and are not, and you have found them *liars* (ψευδεῖς, *pseudeis*, 2:2)." He recognizes that the church at Smyrna has suffered from "the blasphemy of those who claim to be Jews and are not" (2:9) and promises the church at Philadelphia vindication against the same group, "those who claim to be Jews and are not, but *lie*" (ψεύδονται, *pseudontai*, 3:9). At Thyatira, a woman he calls Jezebel "claims to be a prophetess" (2:20), and John implies that she too is a liar in making that claim.

In the later visions, one of the enemies of Christian believers is a beast from the earth who demands worship of the beast from the sea (13:11–18). Subsequently, this second beast is designated as *the false prophet* (ὁ ψευδοπροφήτης, *ho pseudoprophētēs*, 16:13; 19:20; 20:10). A group of 144,000 who stand with Christ the Lamb on Mount Zion (14:1–5) are identified as male virgins who "followed the Lamb wherever he went" (died as martyrs), and as those redeemed from humanity as "firstfruits" of a coming harvest, blameless in that "no *lie* [ψεῦδος, *pseudos*] was found in their mouth" (vv. 4–5). Later, in his vision of a "new heaven and a new earth" (21:1–8), John hears from "the One sitting on the throne" (v. 5) a list of those assigned to "the lake burning with fire and sulfur, which is the second death." The list includes "the cowardly and unbelieving and corrupt and murderers and immoral and sorcerers and idolaters," and ends significantly with "*all the liars*" (πᾶσιν τοῖς ψευδέσιν, *pasin tois pseudesin*, 21:8).[28] The last chapter of Revelation

---

28. The student should notice that the preceding verse explicitly recalls the repeated promises to those who "overcome" in chapters 2–3: "The one who overcomes will inherit these things, and I will be his God and he will be my son" (21:7). This may also explain why the list in v. 8 begins unexpectedly with the "cowardly" (τοῖς . . . δειλοῖς). Although there is no explicit mention of "cowardice" in the seven messages (or anywhere else in the book), "the cowardly" is an appropriate contrast

has a similar list of those excluded from the Holy City: "the dogs, and the sorcerers, and the immoral, and the murderers, and the idolaters, and *everyone who loves and practices lying*" (22:15). In between, John says of the Holy City, "nothing impure shall enter it, nor anyone who *practices corruption or lying* (ποιῶν βδέλυγμα καὶ ψεῦδος, *poiōn bdelygma kai pseudos*), but only those written in the Lamb's book of life" (21:27). The two references to "practicing" or "doing" a lie can be compared to the notion of "doing the truth."[29] What is condemned is not simply telling lies, but living a lie in the sense of living contrary to the values of the author and his community while pretending to uphold the truth. The meaning of *liars* and *lying* is consistent throughout the book.

## The Question of Date[30]

Even when account is taken of possible historical references in the seven messages, little can be said with certainty about the date of Revelation. Most scholars date the book toward the end of the reign of the Emperor Domitian, around 95 or 96.[31] Yet nothing after the brief outbreak of persecution under Nero about 64 begins to match either the violence described in the later chapters of Revelation or the events leading up to it. References to known first-century rulers or events, and especially to specific times of oppression and persecution of Christians in Asia Minor would have made the dating of Revelation an easy matter, but such references are few and

to "the overcomer" (on "cowardly and unbelieving," see the pronouncement of Jesus in Mark 4:40; also 2 Tim. 1:7–8).

29. For "doing the truth," see John 3:21 and references in the Dead Sea Scrolls to members of the community as "those who do truth" (for example, *Manual of Discipline* 1QS 1.5; 5.3, and 8.2, 9).

30. When discussing dates the student should be aware that the designation A.D. (as in A.D. 70), for the Latin Anno Domini ("in the year of the Lord") implies that one writes as a confessing Christian. Those who wish to take a more neutral stance in academic studies increasingly replace A.D. with the letters C.E., which stands for "of the common era," and replace B.C. ("before Christ") with B.C.E. ("before the common era"). Unlike A.D., the designation C.E. goes after the year (as in 70 C.E., as does B.C. and B.C.E.

31. This view goes back to a statement by Irenaeus in the 2d century that John's visions were "seen not long ago, but almost in our own time, at the end of the reign of Domitian" (*Against Heresies* 5.30.3); Eusebius *Ecclesiastical History* 3.18.3.

inconclusive. Consequently, even those who place the book in Domitian's time and base significant conclusions on that dating must admit that the evidence is far from overwhelming.[32] There is, moreover, still a significant minority opinion that dates Revelation as early as 68.[33]

Revelation 17:9–11 offers the best hope of dating the book. An angel interprets for John a vision he has just seen of a prostitute (named "Babylon") seated on a scarlet beast with seven heads and ten horns. "This calls for a mind having wisdom," says the angel; "the seven heads are seven hills, on which the woman sits, and they are also seven kings: five have fallen, one is, the other has not yet come, and when he comes he must remain a little while; and the beast which was, and is not, he is eighth, and [yet] is of the seven, and is headed for destruction." It is generally agreed that the "kings" are Roman emperors, although the Greek word βασιλεῖς (basileis) may refer either to the emperors or to other kings, such as the ten mentioned in 17:12. The identity of the sixth emperor—the one who "is" (reigning at the time of John's vision)—would fix the reign during which the book was written. But does the list begin with Julius Caesar or Augustus? Or does it begin with the first emperor to be hated and feared by Jews and Christians—either Gaius (known as Caligula) or Nero? Another question is: What should be done with the three emperors Galba, Otho, and Vitellius who reigned within the single year 68–69? Should they be counted separately, ignored, or counted as one? The temptation is to contrive a list that leads to a date already assumed on other grounds (or no grounds!).[34]

---

32. See, for example, Hemer, *Letters*, 2–5; Leonard L. Thompson, *The Book of Revelation: Apocalypse and Empire* (New York: Oxford University Press, 1990), 13–15. Thompson finally falls back on the testimony of Irenaeus (see footnote 30).

33. See, for example, Christopher Rowland, *The Open Heaven: A Study of Apocalyptic in Judaism and Early Christianity* (New York: Crossroad, 1982), 403–13; Albert A. Bell, "The Date of John's Apocalypse. The Evidence of Some Roman Historians Reconsidered" in *New Testament Studies* 25 (1978–79): 93–102, and John A. T. Robinson, *Redating the New Testament* (Philadelphia: Westminster, 1976), 221–53.

34. To appreciate how complex this issue is and how inconclusive its results, the student may compare the recent discussions in Thompson, *Revelation*, 14–15; Court, *Myth*, 126–27; Robinson, *Redating*, 242–49; Rowland, *Open Heaven*, 404–6, and the older summary by Isbon T. Beckwith, *The Apocalypse of John* (New York: Macmillan, 1919), 704–11.

One of the most thorough scholarly discussions concludes that "the number seven here is purely symbolical, that the Apocalyptist means to represent the Roman power as a historic whole," and that "who this sixth king, the one reigning at the time, is. . . . must be determined solely by the evidence which the book gives elsewhere of its date."[35] Those who date the Revelation to 95 or 96 during the reign of Domitian, such as Hemer, Leonard Thompson, and John Court, tend to be less dogmatic than those who date it to about 68. With the majority of scholars and the testimony of Irenaeus on their side, their view may stand more or less by default. The minority who favor the earlier date are understandably more vocal. But the question remains open.

Without settling the question of date, the student should keep certain considerations in mind. One is that John's vision of a "new Jerusalem" (21:2; compare 21:9–22:9) suggests that the old Jerusalem has been destroyed by the Romans.[36] This is supported by John's vision in chapter 11, in which he is told that the Gentiles "will trample the holy city for 42 months" (11:2) and, indirectly, by the name *Babylon* given to the city of Rome.[37] There is no hard evidence that *Babylon* was used as a name for Rome before A.D. 70, and the designation appears to be based on an analogy between the ancient world empire that conquered Jerusalem in 586 B.C. and the current world empire that did the same thing.[38] All of this suggests a date after 70. Still, advocates of the early date may argue that even by 68 Jerusalem's fate was so evident that John could write as if it were already accomplished.

A further consideration is that the early date does not allow much time for the development of a certain rumor that is believed

35. Beckwith, *Apocalypse*, 708.

36. In Jewish apocalyptic literature from the same period, compare the vision of the old Jerusalem's transformation in 4 Ezra 9:28–10:28 and its interpretation in 10:29–57 with the Revelation.

37. See 14:8; 16:19; 17:5; 18:2, 10, 21. "Babylon" is clearly identified as Rome in 17:18.

38. The analogy is evident, for example, in the opening lines of 4 Ezra 3, in which "Ezra" has a vision that purportedly refers to Babylon's destruction of Jerusalem in 586 B.C., but actually refers to the events of A.D. 70. The reference to Babylon in 1 Pet. 5:13 could be an exception to the general rule only *if* the designation refers there to Rome, and *if* 1 Peter is dated before 70.

to have inspired some imagery underlying the Book of Revelation. This is the popular Roman expectation of *Nero Redivivus*, or "Nero brought back to life." It is widely thought that Nero, who in 64 became the first great persecutor of Christians is meant by the strange beast of Revelation 17:8 who "was, and is not, and will rise from the abyss and go to destruction." This beast is interpreted by an angel as an "eighth" king, who nevertheless "belongs to the seven" (v. 11), and is commonly identified with the beast in chapter 13, who is said to have received a mortal wound yet lived (13:3, 12, 14). The popular belief was that Nero was not really dead, but would return to take power once more.[39] Advocates of an early date argue that such a rumor could have spread within a very short time,[40] but Nero died in 68, and at least a few years must be allowed for such an expectation to have developed. Hence, the cumulative evidence is against a date before A.D. 70.

The more difficult question is: How long after 70 was the Book of Revelation written? A literal reading of the forty-two months of 11:2 could mean that it was not very long after the fall of Jerusalem, but a consistently literal interpretation of this period in its various expressions throughout the book is difficult to sustain.[41] Hemer, who argues for a date in the time of Domitian, is less confident about his precise dating than about the more general assertion that the book belongs somewhere between 70 and 100, a period about which little is known.[42] This is a wide range, but the student who wants to interpret Revelation probably will have to live with a considerable degree of uncertainty about its date and historical setting.

---

39. The student can read of this expectation in the Roman historians Tacitus (*Histories* 2.8–9) and Suetonius (*Nero* 57), and in a number of Jewish and Christian sources as well: for example, the Jewish *Sibylline Oracles* 4.119–24 and 5.33–34 in James H. Charlesworth, ed., *Old Testament Pseudepigrapha* (London: Darton, Longman, and Todd, 1983), and the Christian *Ascension of Isaiah* 4.2–4 in E. Hennecke and W. Schneemelcher, eds., *New Testament Apocrypha*, Vol. 2 (London: Lutterworth, 1965).

40. Robinson, *Redating*, 245.

41. John writes of "1260 days" in 11:3; 12:6; "a time, times, and half a time" in 12:14, and "42 months" in 13:5.

42. Hemer, *Letters*, 5.

## The Social World of Revelation

The term *social world* has become a kind of catchphrase in biblical studies for the world, not as it actually existed at a given time and place, but as it was perceived by biblical writers and their communities. The methods of sociology have been applied to almost every book of the New Testament, with varying degrees of success.[43] The method as applied to the Revelation has its roots in earlier studies of Christian social history, especially the work of E. A. Judge,[44] but in recent years it has taken on a life of its own in relation to sociological studies of other times and cultures. Judge himself speaks caustically about theories "hammered out in the laboratory of a South-Seas-island anthropologist, and then transposed half-way around the world, and across two millennia, without adequate testing for applicability in the new setting: so powerful is the assumption of the indelible pattern of human social behaviour."[45]

In the case of the Book of Revelation it is important for the student to be aware of sociological theories, despite Judge's warnings, because of the difficulty of assigning the book a date or precise historical setting. Several recent studies are concerned less with the historical and social realities of the church's situation in Asia Minor than with reality as John perceived it. They can be arranged over a kind of spectrum. Some writers presuppose in a rather generalized way that the churches to which John wrote faced persecution in the time of Domitian, yet place the accent on the rhetoric with which

---

43. See, for example, John C. Gager, *Kingdom and Community: The Social World of Early Christianity* (Englewood Cliffs, N.J.: Prentice-Hall, 1975); Gerd Theissen, *Sociology of Early Palestinian Christianity* (Philadelphia: Fortress, 1978); Howard Clark Kee, *Christian Origins in Sociological Perspective* (Philadelphia: Westminster, 1980); Bruce J. Malina, *The New Testament World: Insights from Cultural Anthropology* (Atlanta: John Knox, 1981); Abraham J. Malherbe, *Social Aspects of Early Christianity* (Philadelphia: Fortress, 1983); Bengt Holmberg, *Sociology and the New Testament: An Appraisal* (Minneapolis: Fortress, 1990).

44. See, for example, *The Social Pattern of Christian Groups in the First Century* (London: Tyndale, 1960).

45. E. A. Judge, *Rank and Status in the World of the Caesars and St. Paul* (London: University of Canterbury, 1982), 10; also cited in Hemer, *Letters*, 211–12. See also E. A. Judge, "The Social Identity of the First Christians: A Question of Method in Religious History" in *Journal of Religious History* 11.2 (1980): 201–17.

John persuades his readers to resist,[46] or on his use of "myth" to transcend the harsh realities of the present, rather than on the circumstances of the persecution itself.[47]

Others remain unconvinced that actual persecution enters the picture at all. Adela Yarbro Collins, for example,[48] speaks of a "perceived crisis." She sees real difficulties and anxieties in the position of Christians in Asia at the time of Domitian, arising out of social unrest and tensions both with their Gentile neighbors and with the Jews. Yet she observes that "Revelation does not seem to have been written in response to an obvious, massive social crisis recognized as such by all Christians, not even a regional one."[49] Her view is that the situation faced in the book is not drastically different from that in, say, 1 Peter. The difference is the writer's perception of, and reaction to, that situation.

A much stronger statement of a similar thesis is that of Thompson, who concludes from the lack of evidence for persecution in Domitian's time that the crisis was only in the mind of John and his community. The Revelation is the product of a "cognitive minority" whose "knowledge" of what the world is like conflicts almost totally with the "public knowledge" and values of the society in which it lives.[50] This group was far from representative of all Christians in Asia Minor, and in fact regarded those Christians and Jews who compromised or conformed to Asian society or the Roman Empire as agents of Satan (see Rev. 2:9, 13, 24; 3:9). "Where are the Christian-filled lions?" Thompson asks. "Where is crazed Domitian who sends out his legions against hapless Christians? Where are the oppressed slaves with crosses worn proudly inside their tunics? Where is the crazed seer caught in a state of spiritual madness?"[51] Some readers may feel that Thompson, by insisting that the first

---

46. For example, Elisabeth Schuessler Fiorenza, *The Book of Revelation: Justice and Judgement* (Philadelphia: Fortress, 1985), speaks both of "harassment and victimization" (6) and, more strongly, of "tribulation and persecution" (114). See also her chapter, "Visionary Rhetoric and Socio-Political Situation," 181–203.

47. Gager, *Kingdom and Community,* 50–56.

48. *Crisis and Catharsis: The Power of the Apocalypse* (Louisville: Westminster-John Knox, 1984), chap. 3.

49. Ibid., 98.

50. Thompson, *Revelation.* See esp. his conclusions in chaps. 10–12; see also Collins, *Crisis and Catharsis,* chap. 3.

51. Thompson, *Revelation,* 198.

three of these are missing, has left us with *only* the "crazed seer"! John A. T. Robinson, for example, was quite certain "that the Apocalypse, *unless the product of a perfervid and psychotic imagination* [italics mine], was written out of an intense experience of the Christian suffering at the hands of the imperial authorities, represented by the 'beast' of Babylon."[52]

Some students may be uncomfortable with Thompson and others who seem to divorce the Revelation from real history. Some of us may know individuals in our own time who lead quiet and peaceful lives in prosperous suburban communities, yet who talk constantly of "spiritual warfare," "attacks of Satan," "demonic oppression," and the like, but we are reluctant to think of John as such a person. We prefer to believe he had solid grounds in the real world for his perceptions of the great conflict between God and the devil. When the Revelation is stripped of actual historical references we are tempted to conclude that it is merely the expression of a mood or an eccentric worldview and is not "about" anything. Like the young mathematicians in the Introduction, we are tempted to hear what John is saying without knowing—or caring—what he is saying it about.

There is also the possibility—perhaps equally disturbing to some—that a "naive" approach to Revelation may be right after all, and that what the book is "about" is not the history or "social world" of the writer's time, but the actual future of the world—perhaps of our future. For centuries Christian interpreters have tried to link John's visions to past and present events in the church—the Moslem conquests, the Crusades, the rise of the papacy, and many others.[53] Their forced efforts proved unsuccessful. The application of historical criticism to the Book of Revelation over the last two hundred years has found the key rather in the events of the writer's time. Now this approach too is questioned from the standpoint of sociology and psychology, as well as by those who want to study the book from a purely literary perspective (see pp. 107–127).

---

52. Robinson, *Redating*, 230–31.

53. For full documentation of this tendency up to the mid-nineteenth century, see E. B. Elliott, *Horae Apocalypticae*, 2d ed.; 3 vols. (London: Seeley, Burnside, and Seeley, 1846).

There have always been futurists, whether called enthusiasts, pietists, charismatics, millenarians, or fundamentalists. Before discarding their "naive" approach too quickly, the student should consider carefully whether such an approach might actually be closer to the mind of John than are some of the other options. The student who moves in this direction, however, should ask two hard questions: First, is it possible to transplant John's expectation of an imminent future crisis into our own very different cultural situation and expect it to make sense? Second, if the Revelation *is* about the future of the world, does it shed light on that future as a kind of blueprint or timetable of events to come, or in a more subtle way? Are we to interpret the Book of Revelation literally or symbolically? What, exactly, do those terms mean? These questions are most usefully asked in connection with the interpretation of specific passages.

Although students should familiarize themselves with the historical and social setting of the Book of Revelation in the late first century, this setting is known to us only generally. The book can be dated within about three decades, not three years or one year. If a precise historical setting is the "key" to understanding Revelation, then understanding will elude us. But whatever we may think of the theories of Thompson and of Collins, it is probably true that John's perceptions of his social circumstances are more important for understanding his letter than are the circumstances themselves. These perceptions, fortunately, are also more accessible. Before looking for them in specific passages, the student should give some attention to overall literary, rhetorical, and dramatic structure.

# 3

# Problems of Structure

There is a circular relationship between the literary structure of the Book of Revelation and the interpretation of specific passages: An understanding of the parts is influenced by one's view of the structure of the whole, and a view of structure depends on how certain individual texts are read. The student approaching a particular passage must realize there is no substitute for careful reading and rereading of the whole book in Greek or in various English translations. The next step is to make your own detailed outline of its structure, preferably *before* reading the works of others or the outline I will provide in this chapter. Then as you read this chapter and other discussions, adjust your outline *only* to the extent you are convinced adjustments are necessary. Your own outline should become the one most useful to you, precisely because it is yours. It makes the Book of Revelation your own, and it will be your framework for approaching specific texts—provided, of course, you are willing to revise it in light of what you discover. Because of the complexity of this chapter, you may prefer to postpone reading it until after you have read chapters 4–7.

## The First Vision

If the Book of Revelation is a long prophetic letter narrating a series of visions, the student must know where one vision ends and the next begins. The plurality of John's visions is acknowledged even in the general public's persistent mistitling of the work as the "Book of Revelations." After both a prophetic and an epistolary introduction (1:1–3 and 1:4–6), John begins his first-person narrative with a self-introduction: "I, John, your brother and partner in the tribulation and kingdom and patient endurance in Jesus . . ." (1:9).[1] In a letter of Paul, words like these probably would have appeared in verse 4 as a further designation of "John" who addresses "the seven churches in Asia." Such elaborate self-designations appear in Romans 1:1; 1 Corinthians 1:1; 2 Corinthians 1:1; Galatians 1:1; Ephesians 1:1, and Colossians 1:1.

There is general agreement that the vision narrative introduced at 1:9 extends to the end of chapter 3. John first hears a voice giving him a commission (1:10–11) and then sees the angel-like figure who had spoken to him (1:12–16). Overcome with fear—like many biblical characters confronted with God or an angel—John falls at the figure's feet like a dead man.[2] The figure touches him and identifies itself unmistakably as the risen Christ (1:17–18). What follows in 1:17b–3:22 is one of the longest uninterrupted speeches of Jesus in the entire New Testament. The "I" here is no longer John, but Jesus, speaking with supreme authority as he dictates to John a special oracle for each of the seven churches of Asia.

## John Looks into Heaven

The second vision begins at 4:1, where John again becomes the "I." A reference to "the first voice, which I heard as of a trumpet," echoing 1:10, links this to the preceding vision. But the scene now changes. John sees "a door open in heaven" (or "in the sky")[3] and is told, "Come up here, and I will show you what must happen

---

1. The function of 1:7–8 is not altogether clear. They are not part of the epistolary introduction of vv. 4–6, yet they are preliminary to the account of John's first vision. They are prophetic utterances introduced without any context in a vision, probably intended to make clear from the start the central truths of the coming of Christ and the sovereignty of God. The "yes, amen" of v. 7 appears to echo the "amen" at the end of v. 6.

2. See esp. Dan. 10:7–9 and Ezek. 1:28–2:2; also Gen. 28:17; Exod. 3:6; Luke 1:12–13, 29–30; 2:9–10; Acts 9:4; 10:4; 22:7, and 26:14. The theme of fear and reassurance from God in vision narratives is common in apocalyptic literature.

3. It is often difficult to know whether οὐρανός (ouranos) refers to the dwelling place of God or simply to the sky in Revelation. Here it seems to be the sky because the door into it is visible to John, but from v. 2 on, John is looking into heaven itself.

after this" (v. 1b). As in 1:10 he is "in the Spirit," except that this time he is no longer "on the island called Patmos" (1:9) but in the throne room of heaven itself. Chapters 4–5 can be regarded as one continuous vision of heaven introducing another seven-part series, just as the vision of the resurrected Jesus introduced the seven messages to the churches. The central object in this heavenly vision is "in the right hand of the One seated on the throne, a scroll written both inside and on the back, sealed with seven seals" (5:1). After the Lamb, first announced as "the lion from the tribe of Judah, the root of David" (v. 5), "came and took the scroll from the hand of the One seated on the throne" (v. 7), and after the heavenly celebration of the Lamb's victory (vv. 8–14), the Lamb opens the seals one by one.

Each broken seal, starting at 6:1, introduces a vision. After each of the first four, John "heard" (ἤκουσα, *ēkousa*, 6:1, 3, 5, 7) a voice summoning four horses and their riders one by one, and "saw" (εἶδον, *eidon*, vv. 2, 5, 8) each rider bringing his plague on the earth (6:1–8). After the fifth, John "saw" (εἶδον, v. 9) at the foot of the altar, like a sacrifice, the souls of Christians like himself, "slain for the word of God and for the testimony which they have," crying for vindication and being told to wait until their number is complete (6:9–11). After the sixth, he "saw" (εἶδον, v. 12) the unmistakable signs of the end of the world: the sun darkened; the moon turned to blood; the stars falling, and panic on the earth (vv. 12–17),[4] ending with a cry to the mountains and rocks to "fall on us and hide us from the face of the One sitting on the throne and from the wrath of the Lamb, for the great day of their wrath has come, and who is able to stand?" (v. 17).

## The Problem of Reiteration

The end of chapter 6 raises for the first time a significant question about the structure of the Book of Revelation. Is John's vision of the opening of the sixth seal truly a picture of the end of the world, or of something that will happen before it? If the end of the world, then at

---

4. Compare the last discourse of Jesus (Mark 13:24–27; Matt. 24:29–31; Luke 21:25–27), where such things occur in conjunction with the coming of the Son of Man and the gathering of his elect.

least some of what follows in chapters 7–21 must be regarded as a flashback or reiteration[5] of events preceding the end. This would mean that John's visions are not to be taken as continuous or in chronological sequence. If the sixth seal is *not* a picture of the end of the world, then it may still be possible to arrange the visions chronologically. Commentators on the book divide over this question, with most, perhaps, admitting some degree of reiteration in John's visions. All would agree that John does not simply repeat himself for the sake of repetition, or that he is shown the same thing twice. The reiteration always shows the previous vision in a new way, providing a close-up of some specific aspect not evident before. The issue comes up especially in relating the seven trumpets of chapters 8–9 to the seven bowls of chapter 16 and, to a lesser degree, the seven seals.

Reiteration does not concern the order of the scenes John saw or the order of the book's literary flow. In the context of the vision or narrative, what is seen and told in chapter 6 obviously precedes what is seen and told in chapter 7, which in turn precedes what is seen and told in chapter 8, and so on. No one proposes actually rearranging the visions—at least not in connection with this issue. Reiteration or recapitulation has to do, rather, with *what the visions are about*. Commentators who discuss the matter commonly presuppose that the Revelation is actually about something, presumably the future of the world. They struggle, not to understand the visions as such, but to make sense of the reality to which the visions point. Visions and dreams never quite "make sense," after all, in the way that logic requires. Such commentators are taking seriously the Book of Revelation as "revelation"; this is what most students reading this volume will want to do as well.

Yet we must remember that when we discuss structure we are not yet addressing questions of meaning and reality. The issue of reiteration is not of decisive importance at this stage. The interpreter's first priority is to describe, as clearly as possible, how the order of John's testimony reflects the order of what he had seen and heard. At this point the student will notice that the seventh seal does

---

5. Scholars commonly call this a *recapitulation*, but this term is best avoided because of its rather different use by Irenaeus, in the sense of going over the same ground again with opposite results (as with reference to Christ's reparation of Adam's wrong).

not follow immediately the announcement of the "great day of wrath" at the end of chapter 6. The seventh seal is not broken until 8:1, where John does not say that he *heard or saw anything*—only that "there was silence in heaven for half an hour." The apparent delay of the breaking of the seventh seal, and the equally apparent brevity of what happens—or rather, does not happen—when it is opened, raises questions: (1) What is the status of the intervening material of chapter 7? (2) Is 8:1 all there is to the seventh seal, or does it continue? If it continues, then how far? A third question, not necessarily crucial to the matter of structure yet unavoidable in trying to understand the Book of Revelation, is: When is the seven-sealed scroll actually opened?

## The Problem of Interludes

It has become customary among commentators to speak of Revelation 7 as an *interlude* within the series of seven seals. In much the same way, 10:1–11:13 is frequently described as an interlude within the series of seven trumpets. In both cases the interlude stands just before the last item in the series. Yet no such interlude is evident in connection with the seven churches in chapters 2–3 or the seven bowls of chapter 16. In deciding what it means to speak of *interludes* in the structure of John's visions, the student must recognize that there are no interludes interrupting the visions *as visions*. John does not say to himself at the beginning of chapter 7, "I seem to be entering now into an interlude!" He sees what the seals reveal to him as each is opened. Again it is our twentieth-century concern with what the visions are *about* that leads us to speak of interludes. It is part of the process by which we try to make sense of John's visions in relation to some real or imagined fulfillment that we have in mind.

There is nothing wrong with this, provided we realize what we are doing. As with reiteration, the study of interludes means we take the book seriously. Yet if our goal is simply to trace the intrinsic structure of the Book of Revelation by trying to hear what John heard and see what he saw, there is room to question the need for speaking of interludes. If chapter 7 is not an interlude, then the sixth seal extends all the way from 6:12 through 7:17, and the seventh seal follows immediately in 8:1. Up to this point each description of what happens as the seals break has become progressively longer.

In the case of the sixth seal, according to this reading, the descriptive narrative suddenly becomes a great deal longer. A possible link between the end of chapter 6 and the beginning of chapter 7 can be seen by taking chapter 7 as the vision's answer to the rhetorical question of 6:17b, "Who is able to stand [τίς δύναται σταθῆναι, *tis dynatai stathēnai*]?" Rhetorical questions do not normally require an answer, but the vision of four angels "standing [ἐστῶτας, *hestōtas*] at the four corners of the earth" (7:1), and of an innumerable crowd from all nations "standing [ἐστῶτες, *hestōtes*] before the throne of God and before the Lamb" (7:9), answers it quite aptly and provides a positive contrast to the chaos and despair of 6:12–17. Even if chapter 7 is viewed as an interlude, these observations help explain its placement and its relationship to what precedes.

## The Extent of the Seventh Seal

If chapters 6–7 of Revelation are read without interruption, so that the sixth seal extends from 6:12 through 7:17, what is implied about the seventh seal? Certainly the principle that the material revealed by each of the seals gets longer and longer seems to come to an end with the seventh seal, for "there was silence in heaven for half an hour" is a very short revelation indeed. But is that terse sentence all there is to the last of the seals? The familiar phrase καὶ εἶδον ("and I saw") in 8:2 echoes the language of most of the previous seals (as well as most of the book) and could suggest that the "silence" of 8:1 is merely preliminary to the real revelation of the seventh seal: The temporary "silence" is broken by the sound of the seven trumpets introduced in 8:2 and continuing to the end of chapter 11. If the end of chapter 6 is crucial to one's understanding of the book's structure, the first verse of chapter 8 is even more so. Three alternatives confront the student:

1. The revelation under the seventh seal is the abrupt statement of 8:1 about "silence in heaven," and no more. After the catastrophes of the sixth seal, the reader expects the end—the consummation and the eternal state. But instead there is simply silence. The consummation of all things will come later.

2. The revelation under the seventh seal consists of 8:1–5. The silence is preliminary to "seven angels with seven trumpets," who are introduced but do not actually blow their trumpets (v. 2). Another angel brings to God with incense the prayers of the saints and pours fire on the earth, with "thunders and voices and flashes and an earthquake" (vv. 3–5).

3. The revelation under the seventh seal is the entire series of seven trumpets (8:1–11:19) or, alternatively, all the rest of the book, depending on how one reads the end of the trumpet series in relation to what follows it.

If the first scenario is adopted, there is a full stop after 8:1 and a new beginning. The series of visions that began at 4:1 has ended. This allows, although it does not demand, applying the principle of reiteration, so that the series of seven trumpets is understood as a reenactment of the seven seals. The third option maintains the continuity of John's visions. They emerge from one another like boxes within boxes, or like the graphic "windows" some computer programs allow a user to open within other windows on a screen, or like the joints of a hand-held telescope extended to reveal ever richer detail. The second alternative achieves a kind of compromise in which 8:2–5 both concludes the vision of the seals and introduces the vision of the trumpets.

As in the case of interludes the problem is more ours than John's. Probably neither John nor his first readers and hearers cared much about stops, starts, or reiteration. Even for us, such questions do not come up when we hear the Revelation read or recited orally. Only when we have the written texts in front of us do we have to choose among these alternatives. The choice is crucial *if* our concern extends beyond the visions themselves to the reality to which they refer. If the seven trumpets are *under* the seventh seal, it is commonly inferred, they refer to events or judgments subsequent to those of the seals. They are more distinctly futuristic in that they reveal, not the events leading up to the last day, but the last day itself. If, on the other hand, they are a new and parallel series, then their purpose could be simply to reinforce and intensify the message of the seven seals.

In either case readers will feel the increasing intensity as they move from the seven seals to the seven trumpets. This often brings confusion and frustration as the reader asks, "What can all this possibly be *about*?" The intimations of war, famine, and disease in chapter 6 are one thing. These we are quite familiar with, at least from a distance, through newspapers and television. But what are we to make of locusts with the sting of scorpions, prepared like horses for battle (fifth trumpet)? Or fire-breathing horses with the heads of lions and tails like poisonous snakes (sixth trumpet)? We have no categories for this in our knowledge either of the social history of John's time or of the subsequent history of the church. It is hard for the interpreter not to see all this as distinctly future—and a highly imaginative future at that. The only comparable point of reference in the preceding visions is the sixth seal (6:12–17). Students may find it helpful to regard the trumpet series as a close-up and intensification of the sixth seal—therefore, quite possibly, as part of the seventh! This, however, is for the student to decide.

## The Extent of the Sixth Trumpet

Two similarities between the seals and the trumpets are worth noting. First, in each series the first four are set apart from the last three. The first four seals are the four horses with their riders sent out one by one by the voices of the four living creatures. In the case of the trumpets, the last three are set apart as a series of three "woes" uttered by an eagle flying directly overhead (8:13; compare 9:12, 11:14). Second, as we have seen, it is proposed in both instances that the last item in the series is separated from the previous six by an "interlude."

The interlude here (10:1–11:13) poses as great a problem as in connection with the seals. This can be seen in the placement of the three "woes." The announcement of the woes in 8:13 identifies them with "the rest of the sounds of the trumpets of the remaining three angels." After the fifth trumpet (9:12), John writes, "The first woe is past; behold, two more woes are coming after this." After the sixth trumpet he continues, "The second woe is past; behold the third woe is coming soon." What is significant is that this last announcement comes not after 9:19 or 9:21, at the end of what is usually called the sixth trumpet, but rather at 11:14, after the so-called "interlude."

The placement strongly suggests that John does not regard 10:1–11:13 as an interlude at all, but as part of the sixth trumpet. This is confirmed by the reference in 10:7 to "the days of the sound of the seventh angel, when he is going to blow his trumpet"—a clear reminder to the reader that the trumpet series is still going on and is drawing to its conclusion. In fact it has been hastened by the command *not* to write down "the seven thunders" (10:3–4). John gives the impression that he is passing over another whole series of judgments and is telling only part of what he knows. Consequently, there can be "no more delay" before the "mystery of God" is complete (10:6–7).

The reason many find it necessary to label 10:1–11:13 an interlude is the problem of time reference. If the seven trumpets are depicting the future—not necessarily a distant, but certainly a transcendent future—how can they incorporate something so closely linked to John's own time and experience as his prophetic call (chap. 10), and perhaps the events surrounding the fall of Jerusalem and the destruction of its temple in A.D. 70 (11:1–2)? Again what John is saying must be distinguished from what he is saying it about; the task of discerning the structure should take into account, so far as is possible, only what John explicitly says. When this is done, the continuity between chapters 8–9 and chapter 10 is more easily appreciated.

To John the seven trumpets belong to his own time. Although they point to a future reality on the earth, they are not themselves that reality. Similarly, the strong angel in chapter 10 who gives him a scroll and tells him to "prophesy again" (10:11) belongs to John's current situation. For this reason, John has no difficulty in moving abruptly from the one to the other. Many of us today have a difficulty doing so because we have assigned to chapters 8–9 a future reference (whether literal or symbolic) but have assigned no comparable future reference to the call of John. No one, so far as I know, believes that John is going to return to earth and take the little scroll again from the hand of the strong angel (10:10), eat it, and "again prophesy" (10:11) as he did back in the first century. Chapters 8–9 we assign to the future, chapter 10 to the past. Consequently, we find it difficult to take John's visions as they come, without resorting to interludes.

Yet just as in the case of chapter 7, the material in 10:1–11:13 is placed where it is for a reason. The first six trumpets end on a note of nonrepentance (9:20–21), while the additional material in chapters 10 and 11 ends with the repentance of "the great city, which is spiritually called Sodom and Egypt" (11:8). After a "great earthquake" in which "a tenth of the city fell" (7000 in all), "the rest became fearful and gave glory to the God of heaven" (11:13).[6] Even though the material from 9:13–11:13 is described as "the second woe" (11:14), it has a positive as well as a negative side. Despite all the judgments on the earth and the refusal of its inhabitants to repent, there is a glimmer of hope. God's two witnesses, though slain in the streets of the city before "the inhabitants of the earth" (11:7–10), are vindicated by being raised from the dead (vv. 11–12), and the city turns to God (v. 13). Nonrepentance is not the final word.

## When is the Scroll Opened?

As the trumpet series runs its course, the reader tends to forget the seven-sealed scroll taken by the Lamb in chapter 5 and the seals that are eventually broken. Perhaps even John has forgotten. But questions about it remain. For example, was the scroll opened when the seventh seal was broken, or must that wait until the seven trumpets have sounded? When, if ever, is the scroll actually opened? What does the scroll contain?

A significant feature of the so-called "interlude" in 10:1–11:13 is a scroll John takes from the hand of the strong angel and eats. This scroll is not commonly identified with the seven-sealed scroll of chapter 5, probably because it is designated three times with a diminutive form βιβλαρίδιον (*biblaridion*, "a little scroll," 10:2, 9, 10), instead of the simple βιβλίον (*biblion*, "scroll") used in chapter 5. Yet the fact that it is once called simply "the scroll" (τὸ βιβλίον, 10:8) suggests that the two terms may be interchangeable in this chapter. Possibly it is "little" only in comparison with the giant angel holding it, who stands astride the sea and the earth (v. 2). This strong angel recalls the strong angel of 5:2, while the rainbow at his head recalls the rainbow around the throne of God in 4:3. These echoes of the introductory vision of chapters 4–5 may suggest that the seven-sealed scroll is still in mind.

---

6. See Isbon T. Beckwith, *The Apocalypse of John* (New York: Macmillan, 1919), 592–93, 604. Repentance and "giving glory to God" are explicitly linked in 16:9: "they did not repent so as to give him glory."

The other main characteristic distinguishing the scroll in chapter 10 from the one in chapter 5 is the conspicuous fact that it is not sealed, but "open" (vv. 2, 8). Verse 8 could be interpreted, "Go take *the* scroll [with the definite article recalling the scroll described in chapter 5] now open in the hand of the angel standing on the sea and on the land." If it is the same scroll, then we have the answer to our question. The scroll has been opened somewhere between the breaking of the seventh seal and the blowing of the sixth trumpet.

John learns the content of the scroll by "devouring" it (10:10), not in the metaphorical sense that applies to intense and careful reading, but literally! It tastes sweet in his mouth but bitter in his stomach. John is told by way of interpretation that "You must prophesy again about peoples and nations and languages and many kings" (10:11). Because this is a fairly apt description of what John proceeds to do in chapters 12–20, it is possible to conclude that these subsequent chapters comprise the content of the scroll once sealed with seven seals but now open and revealed. Obviously, such a possibility has a bearing on the structure of Revelation as a whole. It allows John's visions to be seen as a unity in that the plan of God introduced in chapters 1–11 as a heavenly mystery comes to public— even political—realization in the dramatic events of chapters 12–20.

Unfortunately, the identification of the two scrolls with one another, while plausible, is not explicit. John does, after all, introduce "a little scroll" in 10:2, without a definite article, as if he is seeing it for the first time. Possibly the seven-sealed scroll is not opened until the last judgment, when "the scrolls were opened, and another scroll was opened, which is the scroll of life. . . . and anyone who was not found written in the scroll of life was thrown into the lake of fire" (20:12, 15).[7] It is also possible that the Revelation nowhere describes the opening of the scroll because John emphasized the imagery of the breaking of its seals—the things that must happen first—and when he wants to deal with what follows those preliminary things he uses different images. Several alternatives again confront the student.

---

7. Compare "the scroll of life" (3:5; 17:8) with "the Lamb's scroll of life" (13:8; 21:27). It is clear that "the scroll of life" in 20:12, 15 is the same as these, but not so clear whether it is also the scroll taken by the Lamb in chapter 5.

## From the Trumpets to the Bowls

As soon as the third woe is announced (11:14), the seventh angel blows the trumpet. The moment promised with an oath by the strong angel, when "the mystery of God" would be completed (10:5–7) has now come, at least in John's visions: "And there came great voices in heaven, saying 'The kingdom of the world has become the kingdom of our Lord and of his Christ, and he will reign forever and ever'" (11:15). At this, "the 24 elders seated on their thrones before God fell on their faces and worshipped God," praising him for having now asserted his power and sovereignty (vv. 16–18). Then "God's sanctuary in heaven was opened, and the ark of the covenant appeared in his sanctuary, and there came flashes and voices and thunders and an earthquake and great hail" (v. 19). The series of seven trumpets seems to end as it began in 8:5.

But is it the end? If we ignore the interlude, each description in the series has gotten longer than those that came before it, just as in the case of the seven seals. The sixth trumpet, as we have seen, is very long indeed. From this it is possible to argue that the seventh trumpet encompasses part or all of chapters 12–22, just as it was argued that the seventh seal encompassed part or all of chapters 8–22. It appears that the emphasis in 11:15–19 is more on God's victory and vindication than on "woe" or judgment. Consequently, the third woe may consist of more than these five verses. Some have suggested that the third woe is realized only later, in the "seven last plagues" (15:1), or "seven bowls of the wrath of God" (16:1), or perhaps explicitly in the three pairs of woes on Babylon in 18:10, 16, 19. Just as the seven trumpets can be understood as the content of the seventh seal, so it is tempting to link the seven bowls or plagues to the seventh trumpet.

The case is more difficult to make in this instance because so much significant material intervenes between the end of chapter 11 and the introduction of the "seven last plagues" in chapter 15. Almost all outlines of the Book of Revelation recognize a clear break between chapters 11 and 12, and it is probably safer to limit the scope of the seventh trumpet to 11:15–19. At the same time, there are in both the sixth and the seventh trumpets certain anticipations of the latter half of the book. First, there is the possibility that the content of the scroll John eats in chapter 10 (whether or not it is the seven-sealed scroll) is revealed in the visions of chapters 12–20. Second, there are references under the seventh trumpet (11:18) to what will follow in the latter half of the book: to wrath among the nations (chaps. 12–13); to the wrath of God (chaps. 14–19), and to the judgment of the dead, the reward of God's servants, and the destruction of those who have corrupted the earth (chaps. 19–22). None of this, however, quite justifies the conclusion that the seven plagues or bowls represent the content of the seventh trumpet. The relationship between the two series is more complicated than that.

One subtle link between the end of the trumpets in chapter 11 and the introduction of the bowls in chapter 15 is the reference to the opening of God's sanctuary in heaven, and the appearing of the ark of the covenant in the sanctuary (11:19). John's abrupt glimpse into heaven is echoed in 15:5–6 where "the sanctuary of the tent of witness was opened in heaven, and the seven angels who had the seven plagues went out of the sanctuary . . ." This serves to introduce the pouring of the seven bowls of the wrath of God on the earth in chapter 16. It is as if Revelation 15:5 takes up where 11:19 left off. The term *interlude*, if applicable to anything in the Revelation, more appropriately applies to 12:1–15:4 than to the extensions of the sixth seal in chapter 7 or of the sixth trumpet in chapters 10–11. While John probably does not consciously view it as an interlude, 12:1–15:4 does represent a break from the sequences of seven that have dominated John's visions almost from the start.

Yet even this section is structured by its own kinds of enumeration. For example, when seven angels carry out the judgment of God in chapter 14, they are not counted sequentially from one to seven, but in groups of three (vv. 6–12), two (vv. 14–16), and two (vv. 17–20). Another enumeration begins in 12:1, where John picks up the word "appeared" (ὤφθη, *ōphthē*) and the phrase "in heaven" from 11:19, using them as a kind of transition: "And a great sign [σημεῖον, *sēmeion*] *appeared* in heaven, a woman clothed with the sun, and the moon under her feet, and on her head a crown of twelve stars." Two verses later (12:3) he says, "And there *appeared* (ὤφθη) another sign [σημεῖον] in heaven, and behold a great fiery dragon with seven heads and seven horns and on his heads seven diadems." After a succession of encounters and conflicts between the dragon and the woman, and between their respective offspring (chaps. 12–14), a third notice is given in 15:1: "And I saw in heaven another great and marvelous sign [σημεῖον], seven angels with seven last plagues, because in them is completed the anger of God." The three signs seen in 12:1–15:4 serve as the bridge between the seven trumpets of chapters 8–11 and the seven bowls of chapters 15–16.

Within this interlude or bridge, Revelation 15:1–4 has a further transitional function somewhat like that of 8:1–5 between the seals and the trumpets. It is both the conclusion to the three signs of 12:1–15:4 and the introduction to the seven bowls. The seven angels with their trumpets were introduced in 8:2 (perhaps still under the seventh seal). Then, after incense was offered up for the "prayers of the saints" and the "fire of the altar" was poured out on the earth (8:3–5), they sounded their trumpets. Chapter 15 is similar except that there are three steps: First, the angels with the seven last plagues are introduced (15:1); second, they come forth and are given the "seven golden bowls filled with the anger of God who lives forever and ever" (15:7), and, third, they are told to pour out the bowls on the earth (16:1). Here instead of the "prayers of the saints" between the first step and the second, it is the saints themselves (vv. 2–4), now victorious over the Beast who persecuted them in chapter 13.

Several striking parallels between the trumpets and the bowls are traceable to a common dependence on the plagues brought on Egypt in the time of the exodus (Exod. 7–12). Here, if anywhere, a strong case can be made for the principle of reiteration. The first four trumpets are judgments, respectively, on the earth; the sea; the rivers and wells of water, and the sun, moon, and stars (8:7–12). The first four bowls pour the wrath of God on the earth, the sea, the rivers and wells of water, and the sun, respectively (16:2–9). The fifth trumpet and the fifth bowl both bring darkness and pain (9:1–12; 16:10–11). The sixth trumpet and the sixth bowl both bring fearful armies to battle from across the "great river Euphrates" (9:13–21; 16:12–16). The seventh trumpet and the seventh bowl both bring decisive announcements of divine victory (11:15–19; 16:17–21).[8]

The bowls, however, are not simply a rerun of the trumpet series. There is reiteration, but with supplementation and greater intensity. The first four trumpets affect only one-third of the earth; sea;

---

8. For a convenient comparative table, see Glenn W. Barker, William L. Lane, and J. Ramsey Michaels, *The New Testament Speaks* (New York: Harper and Row, 1969), 374.

fresh water; and sun, moon, and stars. The first four bowls contain no such restriction. In the trumpet series, human beings are not injured until the fifth trumpet and not killed until the sixth. In the "seven last plagues" humans are at risk from the start. Most important, several judgments under the seven bowls refer back to the conflict depicted in chapters 12–14 between the followers of Jesus Christ and of the Beast. The first bowl brings "ugly and painful sores" on those "who had the mark of the Beast and who worshipped his image" (16:2; compare 13:16–17; 14:9–10); the third turns rivers to blood because "they have shed the blood of saints and prophets, and you have given them blood to drink" (16:5; compare 13:7, 9–10); the fifth brings darkness not to the sun, but to "the kingdom of the Beast" (16:10–12); the seventh brings destruction to "the great city," or "Babylon the great" (16:19; compare 14:8). No such references are found in the trumpet series, nor are they possible, because "the Beast" and "Babylon" are not introduced until the intervening three great signs in heaven in 12:1–15:4. The student may well come to believe that these three signs are the very heart of the Book of Revelation.

## The Visions of Babylon and Jerusalem

Chapter 17 begins a new vision, built on the seventh bowl and the destruction of "Babylon the great." The new vision is introduced by "one of the seven angels who had the seven bowls," although we are not told which one. The angel said to John, "Come, I will show you the judgment of the great prostitute who is seated by many waters." John writes, "Then. . . . he took me away to the desert in the Spirit" (17:1, 3). At the end of the long vision, John fell at the feet of this angel to worship but was told, "See that you don't do it! I am a fellow servant of you and of your brothers who have the testimony of Jesus. Worship God!" (19:10). Both the introduction and the conclusion are matched in the last vision of the book, where again "one of the seven angels who had the seven bowls" said to John, "Come, I will show you the bride, the wife of the Lamb" (21:9). "Then. . . . he took me away in the Spirit to a great and high mountain, and showed me the holy city Jerusalem coming down out of heaven from God" (21:9, 10). At the end of this vision

John again fell at the angel's feet and was again told, "See that you don't do it! I am a fellow servant of you and of your brothers the prophets. Worship God!" (22:9).

The parallels suggest that the two visions are intended to form a contrasting pair, each centering on a city personified as a woman— Babylon and Jerusalem, prostitute and bride. The first is a "mystery" requiring detailed interpretation by the angel at John's side (17:1–18). The vision leads into a long lament (18:1–24) and finally a song of triumph (19:1–8) over Babylon's fall. The second, anticipated by references to "the marriage of the Lamb," and the Lamb's "wife" at the end of the song over Babylon (19:7, 9), is not a mystery in this sense. The angel simply shows John the glorified Jerusalem in its splendor and allows the vision to speak for itself. The vision of Jerusalem, like the vision of Babylon, is based on what immediately precedes it, in this case the vision (which might have concluded the book) of "a new heaven and a new earth," and of "the holy city, the new Jerusalem coming down out of heaven from God, prepared as a bride adorned for her husband" (21:1–2). The simile, "as a bride adorned for her husband," is transformed in light of the earlier references to the "marriage of the Lamb" into a grand metaphor, "the Bride, the wife of the Lamb" (21:9).

It is impossible to speak of reiteration in this instance because the formal parallels between the two visions only serve to highlight the irreconcilable conflict between the two cities. Yet they are a pair separated by a different kind of vision, just as the seven trumpets and seven bowls were separated by the rather different vision of the three heavenly signs (12:1–15:4). Here again the intervening, unnumbered vision (19:11–21:8) is of major importance in the plan of the book as a whole. These two intervening visions (perhaps the real "interludes" in the Book of Revelation) can be viewed in relation to one another. Three evil figures were brought on the scene in chapters 12–13: (1) the fiery Dragon, identified as Satan (chap. 12), (2) the Beast from the sea (13:1–10), and (3) the Beast from the earth (13:11–17). A fourth figure, Babylon the prostitute, cryptically identified as Rome in 17:18, was introduced in chapter 17. The four are removed from the scene in reverse order: first Babylon (18:1–19:9; her destruction is intimated as early as 14:8 and 16:19); then the two Beasts (now designated as the Beast and the False Prophet) are defeated in battle and thrown into the lake of fire (19:11–21); finally

the Dragon, designated in the same way as when he was first introduced (20:2; compare 12:9) is removed from the scene in two stages
(20:1–10). First he is bound in the "abyss" from which he came (see
11:7; 17:8) for a thousand years (20:1–3); then he is released from
there only to be thrown (after a little more mischief) into the lake of
fire, "where the Beast and the False Prophet are" (20:7–10). While
the Dragon is bound in the abyss, John is given a glimpse of "the
souls of those who were beheaded for the testimony of Jesus and for
the word of God," now seated on thrones and reigning with Christ
for a thousand years (20:4–6). This assurance of vindication for
those who refused to worship the Beast is reminiscent of similar
scenes in 14:1–5 and 15:2–4 and perhaps answers the anguished
prayer of "the souls of those slain for the word of God and for the
testimony they had" in John's vision of the fifth seal (6:9–11).

The thousand-year interval, or *millennium*, whether interpreted
in connection with this vindication of the martyrs or with the
binding of Satan in the abyss, is a point of great contention among
conservative theologians, most of whom are concerned less with
the intrinsic structure of John's visions than with how the visions
are fulfilled. The three solutions most commonly proposed are
labeled *premillennial*, *postmillennial*, and *amillennial* (see pp. 142–
146). These alternatives impinge on the question of structure and
once again raise the question of reiteration. If the events of 20:1–10
simply follow chapter 19, this thousand-year reign of the martyrs
is subsequent to Christ's defeat of the Beast and the False Prophet
and their consignment to the lake of fire—thus, presumably, subsequent to the second coming of Christ. Christ's coming, therefore, is premillennial. But if 20:1–10 simply reiterates the great
conflict between good and evil spanning chapters 12–19, then
either the millennium is now, implying that there is no future millennium at all (amillennialism), or else the events leading to its
realization are already underway, and Christ's coming will follow
it (postmillennialism).

Advocates of reiteration—whether in the interests of an amillennial or a postmillennial approach—consistently point to the fact that
the "millennium" of Revelation 20 ends with an outbreak of evil
and the gathering of armies to battle, just as chapters 12–19 ended
with the great battle of Armageddon mentioned in 16:16 (see also
17:14) and narrated in 19:11–21. Yet again it must be noted that the

question of reiteration comes up only in relation to the *fulfillment* of John's visions, not the visions themselves. The fact that the Dragon is finally consigned to the lake of fire, "where the Beast and the False Prophet are" (20:10) makes it unmistakably clear that *in the context of the visions*, the events of chapter 19 are understood to lie in the past, and that John is not aware of simply going over familiar ground again.

The vision that began at 19:11 concludes with:

the disappearance of earth and sky (20:11),

the judgment of all the dead (20:12–13, 15; compare 11:18),

the consignment of death itself to the lake of fire (20:14),

glimpses of a new sky, a new earth, and a "new Jerusalem" (21:1–2),

explicit assurance from "the One sitting on the throne" that "I am making all things new" (21:5), and

a solemn reminder of the alternatives of life or death (21:3–8).

The effect of all this is to bring to realization the intimations of victory found repeatedly through the book (for example, in the promises to "overcomers" in chapters 2–3; in 7:13–17; 11:15–19; 14:1–5; 15:2–4; 19:1–9, and 20:4–6).

Just as there is a woman in John's vision before the dragon, the two beasts and the prostitute were introduced (12:1–2), so the vision pictures a woman after they are gone (21:2). The first is a mother, the mother of the Messiah; the second is a bride, the wife of the Lamb. The image of the Bride comes to life when the angel discloses to John a glorified Jerusalem, in contrast to fallen Babylon (21:9–22:9). At the end of the vision the angel solemnly assures John that "These words are faithful and true" (22:6), echoing a similar assurance in 19:9b ("These are the true words of God"), and again disclaims any status entitling him to John's worship (22:9). In the immediate setting of each pronouncement, "these words" are the words of the angel who presents to John the respective visions of Babylon and Jerusalem. But in a broader sense they refer to the whole Book of Revelation (compare 22:6–7 with 1:1–3). The "words of the prophecy of this book" are not to be sealed up, for they are about to go into effect (22:10), and nothing is to be added to or taken from them, under penalty of the plagues written in the book, and exclusion from the Holy City (22:18–19).

The structure of the conclusion (22:10–21) cannot be determined with certainty. The angel continues to speak in verses 10–11, but whether the speaker in verses 12–15 is the angel or Jesus is not clear (see p. 96). Jesus, for the first time, identifies himself by name in verse 16, and he continues to speak through verse 20a. John responds in verse 20b on behalf of the Christian community with the invitation, "Come, Lord Jesus," and concludes his letter in what had become the customary Christian manner (v. 21).

## Outline of the Book of Revelation

In light of the preceding discussion, the following is proposed as one possible outline of the Book of Revelation. It is only a sample. Virtually all the problems we have addressed have been resolved by others in other ways, and there are as many different outlines as there are interpreters.[9]

   I. Introduction (1:1–8)
      1. Superscription (1:1–3)
      2. Epistolary introduction (1:4–6)
      3. Words of prophecy (1:7–8)
  II. A Vision of Jesus (1:9–3:22)
      1. The commissioning of John as prophet (1:9–20)
      2. The seven oracles of Jesus Christ (2:1–3:22)
         Ephesus (2:1–7)

---

9. To sample different approaches, see Henry B. Swete, *The Apocalypse of St. John* (London: Macmillan, 1972), xxxiii–xxxv; R. H. Charles, *The Revelation of St. John*, 2 vols., International Critical Commentary (Edinburgh: T. and T. Clark, 1920), 1.xxiii–xxviii; Austin Farrer, *A Rebirth of Images: The Making of St. John's Apocalypse* (Boston: Beacon, 1963), 36–58; Beckwith, *Apocalypse*, 255–91; George R. Beasley–Murray, *The Book of Revelation*, New Century Bible (London: Oliphants, 1974), 29–32; Josephine Massyngberde Ford, *Revelation*, Anchor Bible 38 (Garden City, N.Y.: Doubleday, 1975), xv–xvi; Adela Yarbro Collins, *The Combat Myth in the Book of Revelation*, Harvard Dissertations in Religion 9 (Missoula, Mont.: Scholars, 1976), 5–55; Elisabeth Schuessler Fiorenza, *The Book of Revelation* (Philadelphia: Fortress, 1985), 159–80; A. J. Beagley, *The 'Sitz im Leben' of the Apocalypse with Particular Reference to the Role of the Church's Enemies* BZNW 50 (Berlin: de Gruyter, 1987), 181.

Smyrna (2:8–11)
Pergamos (2:12–17)
Thyatira (2:18–29)
Sardis (3:1–6)
Philadelphia (3:7–13)
Laodicea (3:14–22)

III. A Vision in Heaven (4:1–11:19)
   1. The throne scene (4:1–11)
   2. The Lamb and the scroll (5:1–14)
   3. The seven seals (6:1–8:5)
      The first four seals: four horsemen (6:1–8)
      The fifth seal: souls beneath the altar (6:9–11)
      The sixth seal: wrath and vindication (6:12–7:17)
      The seventh seal: silence and seven trumpets (8:1–5)
   4. The seven trumpets (8:6–11:19)
      Heading (8:6)
      The first four trumpets: on the earth, sea, fresh waters, and the sun, moon, and stars; three woes announced (8:7–13)
      Fifth trumpet/first woe (9:1–12)
      Sixth trumpet/second woe (9:13–11:14)
      Seventh trumpet/third woe: The sanctuary opened in heaven (11:15–19; compare 15:5–8)

IV. A Vision of Signs (12:1–15:4)
   1. "A great sign in heaven": A woman about to give birth (12:1–2)
   2. "Another sign in heaven": The Dragon and his cohorts (12:3–14:20)
      War in heaven (12:3–12)
      War on earth (12:13–14:20)
      The protection of the woman (12:13–13:1)
      The Beast from the sea (13:2–10)
      The Beast from the earth (13:11–17)
      The number of the Beast (13:18)
      The redeemed as "firstfruits" (14:1–5)
      A "harvest" by seven angels (14:6–20)
   3. "Another great and marvelous sign in heaven":
      Seven angels with the seven last plagues and "those who had been victorious over the beast" (15:1–4)

V. A Vision of Plagues (15:5–16:21)
  1. Judgment from the open sanctuary in heaven (15:5–16:1; 15:5 takes up where 11:19 left off)
  2. The first four bowls: on the earth, sea, fresh waters, and sun (16:2–9)
  3. The fifth bowl: on the throne of the Beast (16:10–11)
  4. The sixth bowl: Armageddon (16:12–16)
  5. The seventh bowl: Babylon's fall (16:17–21)
VI. A Vision of Babylon (17:1–19:10)
  1. A revelatory vision by an angel who had one of the seven bowls: The prostitute in a desert (17:1–6)
  2. Interpretation of the vision (17:7–18)
  3. The funeral dirge over Babylon (18:1–24)
  4. A celebration of God's justice (19:1–8)
  5. The angel's testimony and disclaimer (19:9–10)
VII. A Vision of Final Judgment and Victory (19:11–21:8)
  1. The Rider on the white horse (19:11–16)
  2. The judgment of the Beast and his armies (19:17–21)
  3. The judgment of the Dragon (20:1–10)
  4. The general judgment (20:11–15)
  5. The new Jerusalem in a new world (21:1–8)
VIII. A Vision of Jerusalem (21:9–22:9)
  1. A revelatory vision by an angels who had one of the seven bowls: The Bride on a high mountain (21:9–22:5)
  2. The angel's testimony and disclaimer (22:6–9)
IX. Conclusion (22:10–21)
  1. The angel's last words (22:10–15)
  2. The testimony of Jesus (22:16–20a)
  3. John's response (22:20b)
  4. Final exhortation (22:21)

Again, the best outline is the one you have made for yourself. With such an outline in hand, you are ready to approach specific texts, as long as you allow those texts to challenge and amend your outline.

# Part 2

# Specific Examples
# of Exegesis
# in Revelation

# 4

# Text Criticism

No one can interpret a text, ancient or modern, without knowing how the text reads. In the Book of Revelation as in the rest of the New Testament, the student who has some background in Greek will want to use the twenty-sixth edition of the Nestle-Aland *Novum Testamentum Graece*, abbreviated as $N^{26}$.[1] Those who have no knowledge of Greek will use a modern English translation, such as the Revised Standard Version (RSV) or the New International Version (NIV), based on Greek texts very similar (usually identical) to that of $N^{26}$.

As Scot McKnight points out,[2] $N^{26}$ is much superior to the popular United Bible Societies text, 3d ed., abbreviated as $UBS^3$.[3] The latter tells students more than they want, or need, to know about the textual variants it lists but does not list nearly enough of the variants. It claims to be intended for Bible translators, but if a Bible translator could take only one text to the mission field, it is hard to imagine why he or she would choose $UBS^3$ over $N^{26}$. The only real advantage of the UBS is the attractiveness and readability of its type. Possibly the reason for its popularity is that variant readings are classified according to the degree of probability with which the

---

1. Stuttgart, Germany: Deutsche Bibelstiftung, 1979.
2. Scot McKnight, *Interpreting the Synoptic Gospels* (Grand Rapids: Baker, 1988), 47–48.
3. Kurt Aland, et al., eds., *The Greek New Testament*, 3d ed. (Stuttgart, Germany: United Bible Societies, 1983).

editors have adopted them, from "A" (very probable) to "D" (very uncertain). But students (and translators) fall into two main categories: those who are unequipped to evaluate the manuscript evidence for themselves and therefore simply follow the published text, and those who are prepared to evaluate the evidence and therefore decide textual questions for themselves. Neither group will particularly benefit from the inevitably subjective "A–B–C–D" classifications.

McKnight's goal that "students should learn how to determine the original text while recognizing that rarely will they find themselves in disagreement with N[26]" is as appropriate in the Revelation as in the Gospels.[4] The student can gain an appreciation for what modern textual criticism has contributed to our understanding of Revelation simply by comparing certain readings in the King James Version (KJV) with the Greek of N[26], or with a modern English translation, such as the RSV or NIV.

## Examples of Textual Variation

### 1:5b-6

The KJV text reads, "Unto him that loved us, and washed us from our sins in his own blood, and hath made us kings and priests unto God and his Father. . . ." The verb "loved" is based on the aorist (past) participle ἀγαπήσαντι (agapēsanti), but N[26] prefers the present participle ἀγαπῶντι (agapōnti, "loves"). "Washed" is a translation of the participle λούσαντι (lousanti), but N[26] reads instead λύσαντι (lusanti, "loosed" or "freed"). Where the KJV speaks of "kings and priests," N[26] has "a kingdom, priests" (βασιλείαν, ἱερεῖς, basileian hiereis, instead of βασιλεῖς καὶ ἱερεῖς, basileis kai hiereis). Obviously these textual differences do affect meaning to some degree, and in each instance the text found in N[26] is based on stronger manuscript evidence (compare the wording of the NIV translation: "To him who loves us and has freed us from our sins by his blood, and has made us to be a kingdom and priests to serve his God and Father. . . ."

---

4. Ibid., 48.

## 5:9–10

According to the KJV, the four living creatures and the twenty-four elders in heaven fell down before the Lamb, "And they sung a new song, saying, 'Thou art worthy to take the book, and to open the seals thereof: For thou wast slain, and hast redeemed us to God by thy blood out of every kindred, and tongue, and people, and nation; And hast made us unto our God kings and priests: and we shall reign on the earth.'" The first person pronouns "us" and "we" make it clear that these singers are celebrating their own redemption. It is implied that they are (or at least represent in some way) human beings redeemed through Jesus' blood out of all the nations of the world (in some older commentaries the twenty-four elders were taken to represent the total of the twelve tribes of Israel and the twelve apostles of Jesus!).

The text of $N^{26}$ is different. The first person pronouns have disappeared. Instead of redeeming "us to God" (ἡμᾶς τῷ θεῷ, *hēmas tō theō*) in verse 9, the Lamb has redeemed "to God" (τῷ θεῷ) from all the nations of the world. Instead of having made "us for our God kings and priests" in verse 10, the Lamb has made "them [αὐτούς, *autous*] for our God a kingdom[5] and priests." In the same verse, instead of "we shall reign on the earth," the text according to $N^{26}$ is, "they shall reign [βασιλεύ—σουσιν, *basileusousin*] on the earth" (again see the NIV). The four living creatures are singing *about* redeemed human beings, not *as* redeemed human beings, or even as their heavenly representatives. An appreciation of $N^{26}$, and of modern English translations, demonstrates that the "elders" and "living creatures" in the Revelation are distinct orders of angels, and should caution the student to "let angels be angels" without trying to make them symbols of something else.[6]

These two examples illumine for the student the uniqueness of the manuscript tradition in the Revelation. In most of the rest of the

---

5. Notice the same textual variation here as in 1:6: "kingdom" (βασιλείαν, *basileian*) instead of "kings" (βασιλεῖς, *basileis*). One important manuscript omits the phrase, "for our God," altogether.

6. See the thorough and perceptive discussion a generation ago by Ned B. Stonehouse, "The Elders and the Living-Beings in the Apocalypse," in *Paul before the Areopagus and Other New Testament Studies* (London: Tyndale, 1957), 88–108.

New Testament, the beginning student learns to favor readings supported by what was once called the "Neutral" text, represented by the two fourth-century uncial (capital letter) Greek parchment manuscripts, Codex Vaticanus (B) and Sinaiticus (‎א). Students are also taught to watch for and appreciate (not necessarily to adopt) the distinctive readings of the so-called "Western" text, said to be represented in the Gospels and Acts by the fifth-century Codex Bezae and in the letters of Paul by the sixth-century Codex Claromontanus (both listed by modern textual editors as D). The "Western" text is so designated because it is frequently represented in the old Latin versions from western Africa and Europe and in Jerome's Latin Vulgate.

The majority of later Greek manuscripts (from the sixth century to as late as the fifteenth century) exhibit a longer, more elaborate text type sometimes called the "Byzantine" text (because of its dominance in the Byzantine empire) and more recently simply the "Majority" text. This is the type of text underlying the first printed editions of the Greek New Testament (sometimes called the *Textus Receptus*, or "received text," first published in 1556), and consequently the text underlying the KJV.

The picture is quite different in Revelation.[7] Codex Vaticanus breaks off at Hebrews 9:14, and contains nothing of the Book of Revelation. The same is true of the two manuscripts designated as D, for they are limited (respectively) to the Gospels and Acts, and to Paul. Although there are Latin versions of Revelation (as well as Syriac, Coptic, Armenian, and many others), there is no traceable "Western" text. Codex Sinaiticus does contain the entire Book of Revelation, and is an important witness to its text (though far less important than in the rest of the New Testament). More significant, in the judgment of most specialists, is the fifth-century Codex Alexandri-

---

7. Clear, simple discussions of the text of Revelation are not easy to find. Perhaps the best brief statement for the student with some knowledge of textual criticism is in the "Introduction" to N[26], pp. 53–54. See also Isbon T. Beckwith, *The Apocalypse of John* (New York: Macmillan, 1919), 411–16. A longer, though not so clear, discussion can be found in R. H. Charles, *The Revelation of St. John*, 2 vols., International Critical Commentary (Edinburgh: T. and T. Clark, 1920), 1.clx–clxxxiii. For an exhaustive, and truly exhausting, treatment of the subject (over 1400 pages), see H. C. Hoskier, *Concerning the Text of the Apocalypse* (2 vols.; London: Bernard Quaritch, 1929).

nus (A), which also contains the entire book.[8] Codex A is the fore-most Greek witness to the text of Revelation. Other major texts for the Revelation are  C (the fragmentary fifth-century  Codex Ephraemi Rescriptus),Codex ℵ (Sinaiticus), and one Chester Beatty papyrus (p[47], consisting of Rev. 9:10–11:3; 11:5–16:15, and 16:17–17:2). The reason for the very different textual history of the book is the fact that its canonicity was rejected by some segments of the ancient church, so that it was often not copied either with the Gospels or the letters of Paul, or even with the disputed "general epistles" of Peter, Jude, James, and John.[9]

The implications of this textual history for the determination of the correct readings in the two examples given above (Rev. 1:5b–6 and 5:9–10) are not difficult to see. The student has only to look closely at the textual apparatus of N[26], referring when necessary to the "Introduction" for the editors' explanation of their shorthand.[10] Most of the readings supported by the KJV but not by N[26] are based on the so-called "Majority" text. If textual criticism were simply a matter of counting manuscripts (majority-rule), this would be strong support, but the majority texts are late manuscripts, not the earlier, more significant, witnesses discussed above. For example, λούσαντι ("washed") in 1:5b is the reading of the Majority text, with one uncial manuscript (Codex Porphyrianus [P] from the ninth century), and a few noteworthy minuscules (manuscripts written in a cursive script) singled out. A glance at the list of manuscripts in the back of N[26] will show the student that these minuscules (1006, 1841, and others) are not particularly early, ranging in date from the ninth to the thirteenth centuries. The most significant witness for "washed" is P, but arrayed against it are ℵ, A, and C, as well as p[18] (a third- or fourth-century papyrus fragment containing Rev. 1:4–7). It is easy to see why the editors of N[26] decided as they did.[11] The

---

8. Charles, *Revelation* (clxvi) goes so far as to speak of "the absolute pre-eminence of A."

9. See Kurt Aland and Barbara Aland, *The Text of the New Testament* (Grand Rapids: Eerdmans, 1987), 48–50.

10. Pp. 39–72.

11. The same decision was made by the editors of UBS, for reasons given by Bruce M. Metzger, *A Textual Commentary on the Greek New Testament*, corrected (New York: United Bible Societies, 1975), 729.

picture is much the same with the other variants in 1:5b–6, except
that the text behind the KJV lacks even the support of P.

The KJV, and the Textus Receptus behind it, has somewhat stronger evidence in its favor in 5:9, where ἡμᾶς ("us") is found, either
instead of the words "for God" (in the twelfth-century minuscule 1
and certain Vulgate manuscripts), or in addition to those words (in
the Majority text, in Latin and Syriac versions, and most significantly in ℵ). Only A is listed on the other side, though UBS³ adds the
Ethiopic version (p⁴⁷ and C, do not include this section of Revelation). The fact that N²⁶ followed A against virtually all other witnesses is a measure of the confidence the editors have in this manuscript. Their decision, however, may also have been influenced by
the consideration that the longer reading of ℵ and others (ἡμᾶς τῷ
θεῷ, "us for God") could be a late conflation of the two other
options, while the simple ἡμᾶς is rather weakly attested.[12]

The manuscript evidence in support of N²⁶ is more conclusive
in 5:10 than in 5:9. Not even the Majority text, but only a few late
minuscule manuscripts and versions and two patristic citations are
listed in favor of ἡμᾶς ("He has made *us* for our God a kingdom").
As for the reading βασιλεύσομεν (*basileusomen*, "*we* shall reign on
the earth"), it is not so much as listed in N²⁶. The student must turn
to UBS³ to discover that the first person plural is supported by one
late Greek minuscule, one thirteenth-century Latin version, a few
patristic citations, and little else. The interest of N²⁶ is focused
rather on a different problem, the variation between its reading
βασιλεύσουσιν (*basileusousin*, "they shall reign"), supported by P,
a number of minuscules, and the Latin and Coptic versions, and
βασιλεύουσιν (*basileuousin*, "they are reigning"), supported by A,
other minuscules, and the Majority text. The latter question is obviously one of considerable importance for the eschatology of the
Revelation. If the people of God are already a βασιλεία (basileia,
"kingdom" in 1:6; 5:10), does that mean they are reigning on earth
now, or is their reign designated for the future (compare 20:6b;
22:5)?

Such examples clearly show how the meaning of a passage can
hinge on a textual variant. If the four living creatures and twenty-

---

12. For further discussion, see Metzger, *Textual Commentary*, 738, and Stonehouse, "Elders," 98–100.

four elders are not singing about themselves as the redeemed, then it is idle to try to identify them with Jews, Christians, a chosen remnant, or Christian martyrs. They are what they appear to be—angelic figures who are part of the setting of John's vision of the throne room of heaven, and who celebrate the victory of Jesus Christ on behalf of his people. Moreover, the question of whether the people of God are reigning on earth now or in the future will inevitably have a bearing on the interpretation of the promise in chapter 20 that those who have a part in the "first resurrection" will be "priests of God and Christ and will reign with him for a thousand years" (20:6).

Several other case studies in the text of the Revelation are worthy of special mention.[13]

### 12:18–13:1

The KJV begins chapter 13 of Revelation with the words, "And I stood upon the sand of the sea, and saw a beast rise up out of the sea, having seven heads and ten horns, . . ." The translation, "I stood," is based on the Greek ἐστάθην (*estathēn*) supported by the Majority text, two or three late uncials, some Vulgate manuscripts, and one or two other versions. N[26] has instead ἐστάθη (*estathē*, he stood), referring to the Dragon of 12:13–17. This reading has the support of P[47], ℵ, A, C, several later minuscules, and most of the Latin witnesses.

Although only one Greek letter is involved, the difference for the story line of Revelation is considerable. The text of N[26] accents the close link between the Dragon of chapter 12 and the Beast of chapter 13, and the character of the two chapters as successive rounds in a single conflict (see p. ooo). "He stood" means that the Dragon, frustrated in his attempt to destroy the woman who bore the child, begins his war against "the rest of her offspring" (12:17) by standing at the sea and (presumably) raising up the Beast from the sea to do his evil work. The statement in question is transitional, but because it temporarily concludes the Dragon's activity, it belongs with chapter 12, being numbered as 12:18. The text behind the KJV, on the

---

13. See also B. F. Westcott and F. J. A. Hort, *The New Testament in the Original Greek: Introduction and Appendix* (London: MacMillan, 1896), 136–40.

other hand, concludes its description of the Dragon's activity at
12:17 and assigns to John an abrupt reference to his own geographical position (on Patmos?) as he watched the Beast with seven heads
and ten horns rise out of the sea. ἐστάθην ("I stood") sets the stage
for καὶ εἶδον ("and I saw, 13:1), and belongs with chapter 13.
Because it is a matter of a single letter, it is difficult to be absolutely
certain, but the manuscript evidence in favor of the text of N[26] is
overwhelming.[14]

### 15:6

By this time students may tend to conclude that one never, never
disagrees with N[26]. The better principle is "hardly ever." According
to the KJV of Revelation 15:6, "the seven angels came out of the temple, having the seven plagues, clothed in pure and white linen, and
having their breasts girded with golden girdles." In this case, N[26] is
basically in agreement. The word for "linen" is the noun λίνον
(*linon*) which means "flax" or anything made from flax, such as a
lamp wick, a net, or a garment (the NIV has the angels "dressed in
clean, shining linen"). But a glance at the textual apparatus in N[26]
shows that the support for this reading is rather slight. p[47], for
example, along with one late uncial and a few minuscules and Latin
versions, has instead the equivalent adjective λίνουν (*linoun*) "made
of linen." ℵ has the same word differently (according to UBS[3],
λίνους [*linous*], in the nominative case). More strikingly, the two
best witnesses to the text of Revelation (A and C), along with one or
two minuscules and some forms of the Vulgate, have the word
λίθον (*lithon*, "stone") in place of λίνον.

Again it is a matter of only one letter. Not only the manuscript
evidence, but the principle often invoked that the more difficult
reading is apt to be the correct one, suggests that λίθον deserves a
close look from any student working on this passage. "Seven angels
clothed in pure, shining stone," is, if nothing else, a "difficult" reading. It was not too difficult for the Wycliffe translation of 1380 or the
Rheims New Testament of 1582, both of which adopted it, but it is
rejected by all modern textual editors. UBS[3] agrees with N[26] in

---

14. The "C" rating given to this variant in UBS[3] is perhaps unnecessarily cautious.

favoring the traditional λίνον, and with a surprisingly strong "B" rating. N[26] cites Ezekiel 28:13 as a parallel to, and possible source of, the reading λίθον, but Metzger considers this a "superficial parallel" and the reading a "transcriptional error that . . . makes no sense."[15]

The parallel is indeed superficial, although it does employ the strange metaphor of "clothing" oneself (in the sense of being adorned) with precious stones of every kind. But it is not quite true that the reading makes no sense. As part of a vision it may have been intended either to recall John's vision of a throne and of "the One seated, similar in appearance to jasper stone and carnelian" (4:3), or to anticipate his later vision of the Holy City, "having the glory of God, its splendor like a most precious stone, like jasper sparkling as crystal" (21:11; compare vv. 18–19). With such texts in mind, it is possible to imagine "clothed in pure shining stone" as simply a way of saying that the seven angels were clothed in the glory of God. If λίθον was the original reading, it is easy to see how, by changing just one letter, a scribe might have written λίνον, and so "improved" the sense, perhaps in light of four references elsewhere in Revelation to "fine linen" (18:12, 16, and twice in 19:8, using John's characteristic term, βύσσινου [bussinou]). Other scribes might then have changed λίνον to the more common spelling λίνουν. On the other hand, if λίνον was original, it is difficult to see why any scribe would have changed it to λίθον. The latter is a reading that explains quite well how all the others came into being.

The point of this discussion is not to argue that the question is closed, but on the contrary, to suggest that in spite of the agreement among the KJV, N[26], UBS[3], and all modern translations with which I am familiar, it is still very much open. Students should not allow their high respect for N[26] to turn into reverence.

### 2:20

Other readings rejected by N[26] and UBS[3] are intriguing even when the student may properly hesitate to adopt them. In the message to the church at Thyatira, Jesus tells the "angel" of the church, "I have against you that you tolerate the woman, Jezebel, who calls

---

15. Metzger, *Textual Commentary,* 754.

herself a prophetess, and teaches and deceives my servants into immorality and eating food sacrificed to idols" (2:20). The sense of the verse is about the same in KJV, N[26], UBS[3], and the modern translations. But certain manuscripts insert the pronoun σου (*sou*, "your") between τὴν γυναῖκα ("the woman") and the name, "Jezebel."

The effect is startling. With the pronoun, τὴν γυναῖκα σου, *tēn gunaika sou*, means "your wife." The "angel" of the church is apparently understood to be a church leader, perhaps the bishop or pastor, and it is made to sound as if the pastor's wife is the one causing all the trouble! The manuscript support for this reading is far from negligible (A, the Majority text, including some notable minuscules, the Syriac, and Cyprian), and the student should look at it carefully. Still, it is out of character for the "angel" to be addressed as an individual, apart from the congregation as a whole. Metzger is probably right in suggesting that a later scribe became confused at the repeated occurrences of σου in verses 19–20 (four examples of "you" or "your," not counting the one in question), and placed one where it did not belong.[16]

These examples demonstrate some of the appeal of textual criticism, even to the nonspecialist. Although many textual variants come under the heading of minutiae, others affect the meaning of the text in significant ways. No matter what passage is under consideration, the student will want to take careful note of how the text reads, what the variants are, and why the text of N[26] is to be preferred—if in fact it is! The student is then ready to begin the task of exegesis.

---

16. Ibid., 734.

# 5

# Grammar and Style

Students must pay attention to the grammar of the Book of Revelation for all the same reasons they pay attention to the grammar of any other book in the Greek New Testament.[1] For example, it will be helpful to notice John's use of the definite article when introducing an object or a figure in his visions. This *article of previous reference* or *anaphoric definite article* is a signal that this is something with which John assumes his readers are familiar, either from an earlier vision, an older text, or from tradition.[2] Beyond "normal" grammar, however, those who have had a year or more of New Testament Greek will quickly discover that the Greek of the Revelation is (to put it mildly) very strange.[3]

---

1. See, for example, Scot McKnight, *Interpreting the Synoptic Gospels* (Grand Rapids: Baker, 1988), 51–56; Thomas R. Schreiner, *Interpreting the Pauline Epistles* (Grand Rapids: Baker, 1990), 77–96.

2. For example, the seven spirits, 1:4; the seven angels, 8:2; the rainbow, 10:1; the beast, 11:7; the war, 16:14. See the discussion in pp. 60–61, regarding the scroll in 10:8, and David E. Aune, "Intertextuality and the Genre of the Apocalypse," Society of Biblical Literature Seminar Papers (1991): 144.

3. Its strangeness was mentioned by Dionysius, Bishop of Alexandria, in the third century (Eusebius *Ecclesiastical History* 7.25–27). In modern times, see the classic discussion, "A Short Grammar of the Apocalypse" in R. H. Charles, *The Revelation of St. John*, 2 vols., International Critical Commentary (Edinburgh: T. and T. Clark, 1920), 1.cxvii–clix, and the recent survey by Stanley E. Porter, "The Language of the Apocalypse in Recent Discussion" in *New Testament Studies* 35.4 (1989): 582–603. On the Hebraic character of John's grammar and style, see Steven Thompson, The Apocalypse and Semitic Syntax (SNTS Monograph Series 52; Cambridge University Press, 1985), and for a differing perspective, Daryl D. Schmidt, "Semitisms and Septuagintalisms in the Book of Revelation," *New Testament Studies* 37.4 (1991): 592–603.

## Grammatical Abnormalities

### 1:4–5

As early as the letter's opening greeting, the student will encounter a striking example of odd grammar: "Grace and peace from the One who is and who was and who is to come" (ἀπὸ ὁ ὢν καὶ ὁ ἦν καὶ ὁ ἐρχόμενος, *apo ho ōn kai ho ēn kai ho erchomenos*, 1:4). The preposition ἀπό (*apo*, "from") requires a genitive object, as in Paul's letters (ἀπὸ θεοῦ πατρὸς ἡμῶν καὶ κυρίου Ἰησοῦ χριστοῦ, *apo theou patros ēmōn kai kyriou iēsou christou*, "from God our Father and the Lord Jesus Christ"). Instead, the objects of the preposition—ὁ ὢν, (*ho ōn*), ὁ ἦν (*ho ēn*) and ὁ ἐρχόμενος (*ho erchomenos*)—are in the nominative case. The explanation commonly given is that of R. H. Charles: "The Seer has deliberately violated the rules of grammar in order to preserve the divine name inviolate from the change which it would necessarily have undergone if declined."[4] A more polite—but also more accurate—way of saying it is that the whole expression, "the One who is and who was and who is to come," functions as an indeclinable noun.[5] Ὁ ὢν (*ho ōn*, "the Existing One," or "the One who is") is the name of God according to the Septuagint (Greek Old Testament) translation of Exodus 3:14, where the Hebrew אֶהְיֶה אֲשֶׁר אֶהְיֶה (*ehyeh aser ehyeh*, "I am who I am") is rendered in Greek as ἐγώ εἰμι ὁ ὢν, (*egō eimi ho ōn*, "I am the One who is").

If John were a grammatical purist, he might have written ἀπὸ τοῦ ὁ ὢν (*apo tou ho ōn*), using the genitive article τοῦ to bracket the whole expression as if it were a proper name. But John is far from a purist. Within the same expression he uses a finite verb as if it were a participle (ὁ ἦν, *ho ēn*, "the One who was") because Greek has no past participle of the verb "to be." He could not have used ὁ γενό–μενος, ("the One who came to be"), as Charles supposes,[6] because it would have contradicted ὁ ὢν and destroyed John's point that God is the eternally existent One. Possibly John could have appealed for justification to the fact that ὁ ἦν (with ὁ accented as a

4. Charles, *Revelation*, 1.10.
5. Isbon T. Beckwith, *The Apocalypse of John* (New York: Macmillan, 1919), 424.
6. Charles, *Revelation*, 1.10.

relative pronoun instead of a definite article) is perfectly good Greek for "that which was" (see 1 John 1:1, "that which was from the beginning"). Obviously he would not have wanted to picture God as neuter (any more than as changing or as coming into being), but he may have felt that the masculine participles ὁ ὤν and ὁ ἐρχόμενος were sufficient to prevent any misunderstanding along that line. In any case, theological meaning and rhetorical style took precedence over concern for the niceties of proper grammar.

In the next two prepositional expressions (vv. 4b–5), John returns to normal usage by putting "the seven spirits" and "Jesus Christ" in the genitive case after ἀπό. In good Jewish fashion, only God is seen as eternal and unchanging. Yet when he attaches to "the seven spirits" a relative clause ("which are before his throne"), the relative pronoun ἅ, according to N[26], is in the nominative instead of the genitive plural.[7] And when he designates "Jesus Christ" as "the faithful witness, the firstborn of the dead, and the ruler of the kings of the earth," the titles all bear the definite article ὁ in the nominative case, not the genitive. This is irregular in New Testament Greek, but not in the Greek of Revelation.

The opening greeting illustrates John's habit of shifting to the nominative case almost by default in appositional and participial phrases, in violation of normal rules of agreement.[8] This occurs with the singular participle λέγων (legōn) and plural participle λέγοντες (legontes, "saying") before certain quotations (4:1; 5:12; 11:15; yet compare 11:12). Sometimes John's abrupt shifts are in different directions: in 21:9 a genitive plural participle (τῶν γεμόντων, tōn gemontōn, "filled") appears where an accusative plural is required. Charles calls this an "oversight,"[9] yet it is a natural one in view of three genitive plural endings preceding and three following, all in a single verse.

---

7. It should be noted that some good manuscripts (‭א and A) read instead the genitive plural article (τῶν, tōn), but this reading is suspect, precisely because it improves John's grammar.

8. See this practice in reference to Antipas, 2:13; Jezebel, 2:20; the new Jerusalem, 3:12; the 144,000, 7:4; the sea creatures, 8:9; the angel with the sixth trumpet, 9:14; the saints, 14:12, and the Dragon, 20:2.

9. Charles, *Revelation*, 2.56.

### 11:1–13

The uniqueness of this passage has often been noted.[10] In 11:1 the participle λέγων is used with no specific antecedent (literally, "there was given to me a reed, like a measuring rod, *saying*, 'Go and measure the temple of God,' . . ."). This dangling participle introduces a narrative of considerable length and significance about the "two witnesses" and their fate (11:1b–13). For a moment this impersonal narrator takes on personality ("*I* will give to *my* two witnesses, and they shall prophesy," v. 3), suggesting that the voice is God's, but through the rest of the account "he" (or "she" or "it") simply tells a story. John never actually *sees* the two witnesses, or anything that happens to them (the characteristic phrase, καὶ εἶδον, "and I saw," is noticeably absent).

What John records is a prophecy, not a vision. In the course of this prophecy the moods change from imperative (vv. 1–2a) to indicative (vv. 2b–13). The tenses change, sometimes abruptly, from future (vv. 2b–3) to present (vv. 4–6, identifying the "two witnesses"), to a mixture of the future and futuristic present (vv. 7–10), and then abruptly to the aorist, as if John is recounting a vision (vv. 11–13). This is explainable on the ground either that, without having told us, he *is* in fact narrating a vision,[11] or (more likely), he has shifted in Hebraic fashion to the aorist tense with a future meaning, like the Hebrew prophetic perfect.[12]

### 10:7

The prophetic perfect, often used after "and" (with καί in Greek functioning like the Hebrew waw-consecutive), is probably what underlies 10:7: "But in the days of the voice of the seventh angel,

---

10. Ibid., 1.cxxiii, 269–73. Charles attributes its uniqueness to John's use of a source. Given the general peculiarity of the book's grammar and style, this would be difficult to prove.

11. This assumption lies behind the reading ἤκουσα (*ēkousa*, "I heard") in v. 12 (p[47], the Majority text, a later editor of a, certain old Latin versions, one Syriac version, the Coptic, and some ancient commentators), instead of the better attested ἤκουσαν ("they heard"), supported by ‭א‬, A, C, and others, and adopted by N[26]. This is another example of how text criticism impinges on grammar and meaning (see chap. 4).

12. Charles, *Revelation*, 1.cxxiii.

when the trumpet is going to sound, then shall be completed [καὶ ἐτελέσθη, *kai etelesthē*, literally, "and has been completed"] the mystery of God" (see ἐτελέσθη in 15:1).[13]

The issue of "Hebraisms" in the Book of Revelation is much discussed and not yet resolved. Few scholars would argue that the book was written in Hebrew and translated into Greek, yet most assume that the author writes in Greek as a second language and is still thinking in Hebrew.[14] Specifically, the language of Revelation exhibits the blunt, elliptical, and consequently mysterious character of Jewish apocalyptic and Christian prophecy. The author writes as if he were a simple Hebrew Christian transcribing faithfully and without elaboration what he has seen and heard, however fantastic and jarring it might seem to his readers. Whether this is the sober truth or a literary pose is something students will have to decide for themselves. The burden of proof is on those who opt for the latter.

The student should not conclude, however, that the Greek of Revelation totally differs from the Greek of the rest of the New Testament, as if a person had to learn a new dialect of Greek in order to study this book. On the contrary, intermediate Greek students will find Revelation one of the easier New Testament books to read once they have acquired a feel for its distinctive style and vocabulary. It may not be quite as easy as the Gospel or Epistles of John, but it is easier than the Synoptic Gospels and easier than most passages in Paul. "Odd" Greek does not mean exceptionally difficult Greek. The Hebrew roots of John's style give his language a certain simplicity and bluntness for which the student will be grateful.

## Grammar and the Flow of Thought

### 20:4

Despite Revelation's grammatical irregularities, students who find it helpful to diagram or make sentence flow charts of New Testament passages should be able to do so here as easily as anywhere

---

13. Beckwith, *Apocalypse*, 582–83.
14. Charles, *Revelation*, 1.cxlii–clii.

else.[15] This can be done in a three-column format in which the subject of the sentence appears in the left column, the verb (if separable from the subject) in the center column, and the direct object in the right column. Dependent adjectives, participles, and clauses are shown by careful and consistent indentation. This can be illustrated from one of the most controversial verses in the Revelation, in which John sees a group who "lived and reigned with Christ a thousand years." The main pitfall to be avoided is the assumption that such a chart will by itself solve all the problems of this much discussed passage. The Greek of Revelation 20:4 can be laid out as follows:

| | Subject | Verb | Direct Object |
|---|---|---|---|
| 1 | Καὶ εἶδον | | θρόνους, |
| | And I | saw | thrones, |
| 2 | | | καὶ ἐκάθισαν ἐπ' αὐτούς, |
| | | | and they sat on them, |
| 3 | | | καὶ κρίμα ἐδόθη αὐτοῖς, |
| | | | and a judgment was given for them, |
| 4 | | | καὶ τὰς ψυχὰς τῶν πεπελεκισμένων |
| | | | and the souls of those beheaded |
| 5 | | | διὰ τὴν μαρτυρίαν Ἰησοῦ |
| | | | for the testimony of Jesus |
| 6 | | | καὶ διὰ τὸν λόγον τοῦ θεοῦ, |
| | | | and for the word of God |
| 7 | | | καὶ οἵτινες οὐ προσεκύνησαν τὸ θηρίον |
| | | | and such as did not worship the Beast |
| 8 | | | οὐδὲ τὴν εἰκόνα αὐτοῦ |
| | | | nor his image |
| 9 | | | καὶ οὐκ ἔλαβον τὸ χάραγμα |
| | | | and did not receive the mark |
| 10 | | | ἐπὶ τὸ μέτωπον |
| | | | on the forehead |
| 11 | | | καὶ ἐπὶ τὴν χεῖρα αὐτῶν· |
| | | | and on their hand; |
| 12 | | | καὶ ἔζησαν |
| | | | and they lived |

---

15. For more about diagraming, see Gordon D. Fee, *New Testament Exegesis: A Handbook for Students and Pastors* (Philadelphia: Westminster, 1983), 60–77.

| 13 | καὶ ἐβασίλευσαν |
|----|----------------|
|    | and reigned |
| 14 | μετὰ τοῦ Χριστοῦ |
|    | with Christ |
| 15 | χίλια ἔτη· |
|    | a thousand years. |

The chart reveals that the entire verse is the object of καὶ εἶδον, "I saw" (in effect, though not in a strictly grammatical sense). Nothing else appears in the left column. This is the case even when there is no object expressed by the accusative case, as there is in lines (1) and (4). In line (7) John has shifted (in typical fashion for him) to the nominative case (καὶ οἵτινες, kai hoitines) to characterize further the group or groups in view. This shift governs lines (7) through (11).

In line (2) there is no noun or pronoun, accusative or nominative, for the group John "saw," only an indefinite "they" expressed within a verb (καὶ ἐκάθισαν, kai ekathisan, "and they sat"). Possibly John's use of καὶ with the indicative instead of with a more complex participial construction (for example, τοὺς καθημένους, tous kathēmenous, "the ones seated") could be attributed to the influence of Hebrew, yet participles are surely as much at home in Hebrew grammar as in Greek. More likely, John wants to call attention first to actions rather than persons—they "sat" (or "took their seats"), line (2); "a judgement was given for them," line (3).[16] The only noun or pronoun he has used for the group in question up to this point is αὐτοῖς (autois, "for them") in line (3), and he has used it rather casually, inviting confusion with the ἐπ᾿ αὐτούς (autous, "on them") of line (2), referring to the thrones. Only in lines (4) through (11), does John turn his attention to who "they" are, and this he spells out at some length—though not altogether clearly, as the student will discover. In lines (12) through (15) he resumes his list of actions: "they lived" (or "came alive"), and "they reigned with Christ a thousand years." The reader could move directly from the

---

16. An example of this emphasis on action comes in John's first vision of heaven. In 4:2 "a throne was placed" (θρόνος ἔκειτο, thronos ekeito) but the identity of the one who is at the center of the action is ambiguously expressed by a participle without the definite article: καθήμενος (kathēmenos, "[someone] sitting"). Only in v. 3 is the One "sitting" defined by an article (ὁ καθήμενος) and further described.

first three lines of the flow chart to the last four without being aware of anything missing.

The limitations of grammatical analysis are evident in the intervening lines (4) through (11). These lines link the vision of the thousand-year reign with preceding visions. Lines (4) through (6), "The souls of those beheaded for the testimony of Jesus and for the word of God," recall the fifth seal (6:9–11) in particular, as well as several other references to what seems to be at stake throughout, "the word of God," and "the testimony of Jesus" (see 1:2, 9; 12:17; 19:10). Lines (7) through (11), "and such as did not worship the Beast nor his image and did not receive the mark on the forehead and on their hand," recall a number of previous references in the latter half of the book to worshipping the Beast's image and receiving the Beast's mark (13:15–17; 14:9, 11; 15:2; 16:2; 19:20).

What neither our grammatical analysis nor our sentence flow chart can tell us is whether John regards those "beheaded for the testimony of Jesus" and those who "did not worship the Beast" as the same group. If they are not the same, then those who reign during this millennium include both the martyrs (those killed for their faith) and the confessors (those faithful to their Christian confession who did not die). If the same group, then a variety of conclusions might be drawn, among them: *only* Christian martyrs will reign during the millennium while others must wait until the end of the thousand years; *all* Christians will be martyred and consequently will reign with Christ, *or* the second expression somehow interprets the first, so that faithfulness and willingness to die counts with God as martyrdom. Most commentators choose the last conclusion for theological reasons, suggesting that the question is not likely to be settled on grammatical grounds alone (see chap. 8).

### 13:8

Another example of the value of a sentence flow chart is a verse in chapter 13 that has shaped the vocabulary of preachers and theologians who speak of "the Lamb slain [or Christ crucified] before the foundation of the world." What is usually meant is that the provision of Christ's death on the cross as a sacrifice for sin was God's intent from all eternity. Such a belief is not to be faulted (see, for example, 1 Pet. 1:19–20), yet there is room to doubt that it is taught in Revelation 13:8. This can be shown by a very simplified sentence flow chart in English, omitting all unnecessary words:

| | Subject | Verb | Direct Object |
|---|---|---|---|
| 1 | All | will worship | him |
| 2 | | | whose name is not written |
| 3 | | | in the scroll |
| 4 | | | of life |
| 5 | | | of the lamb |
| 6 | | | slain |
| 7 | | | from the foundation |
| 8 | | | of the world |

This is one way to diagram the sentence. The question is what to do with the phrase, "from the foundation of the world," lines (7) and (8). I have placed the phrase in the column directly under the words "is not written" in line (2). The meaning, consequently, is that from the foundation of the world the Beast's name is not written in the slain Lamb's scroll of life. The alternative is to place the phrase in question under the participle "slain" in line (6). This yields the commonly cited theological conclusion that the Lamb, Jesus, was "slain from the foundation of the world."

While the latter interpretation seems more natural from the word order, the former is supported by a somewhat parallel passage, 17:8b. This half verse can be diagramed as follows:

| | Subject | Verb | Direct Object |
|---|---|---|---|
| 1 | the dwellers on earth | will marvel | |
| 2 | whose name | is not written | |
| 3 | | | in the scroll |
| 4 | | | of life |
| 7 | | from the foundation | |
| 8 | | of the world | |

Here the "slain Lamb" is not in the picture at all, and the phrase, "from the foundation of the world," lines (5) and (6), belongs unmistakably in the column under the words, "not written," in line (2). "From the foundation of the world" is simply a way of underscoring the nonelection of "the dwellers on the earth." In a similar way, the diagram given above of 13:8 suggests that the phrase is

John's way of underscoring the nonelection of the Beast, for the Beast and the "dwellers on the earth" (the unbelievers) will share the same fate (see 19:20; 20:15). The "slain Lamb" is mentioned in 13:8 only to identify further the "scroll of life" in which the name of the Beast is not written (see 3:5; 20:12, 15; 21:27).

The grammatical analysis and the sentence flow chart in these examples focus the student's attention on the problem, rather than on its solution. The word order of 13:8 points in one direction and the analogy between 13:8 and 17:8b in another. The issue, like most in Revelation, cannot be conclusively resolved on grammatical grounds alone, yet no one can interpret the book without attending to its grammar and style. No one would call the Revelation's Greek the "best" in the New Testament (whatever that might mean), but students should learn to treat the author's distinctive language with respect. More often than not, if readers are patient, they will discover reasons why words are used as they are.

# 6

# Narrative Criticism:
# The Voices of the Revelation

What is sometimes called the "literary criticism" of the Bible has a number of different aspects when applied to a book such as Revelation. We have dealt with one major aspect in discussing literary genre (chap. 1), with others in connection with the book's visionary structure (chap. 3) and its grammar and style (chap. 5), and we will deal with still others in a later discussion of "intertextuality," or the use and rewriting of earlier traditions (chap. 7).

One major issue remains: the narrator and narrative voices in the Book of Revelation. Whose voices are we hearing as we make our way through the visions that comprise the book? *Narrative criticism* is one branch of *literary criticism*. Whatever else it is, this letter, prophecy, or apocalypse is narrative. Someone tells a story, and through much of the book runs an identifiable story line. Traditional literary criticism asks about the *author* of a work. More recent literary criticism contents itself with asking about the *implied author*. This means the author as understood "from the inside," within the literary framework of the book itself. The implied author of Romans, is "Paul, servant of Jesus Christ, called apostle, set apart to the gospel of God" (Rom. 1:1). From Paul's other letters and the Book of Acts we know who this "Paul" was, but the notion of implied author puts this "outside" information off limits, and confines itself to Paul as revealed in Romans alone.

This may seem a rather silly self-limitation, like fighting with one hand tied behind us. If we have additional information about Paul, why not use it? In the Book of Revelation, however, as we saw in chapter 1, the implied author is all we have. Outside information does not allow positive identification of John beyond what he himself reveals to his readers: He is "your brother and companion in the tribulation and kingdom and patience in Jesus" (1:9). We can infer that he was a prophet (19:10; 22:9, 16) with a ministry to a number of churches (1:9–11; 22:16), but that is about all. There is no useful distinction here between author and implied author.

## The Narrator(s)

Through much of the Revelation, the implied author is also the narrator, as in 1:9–17a. But in the middle of verse 17 a human figure "like a son of man," who has appeared to John in his opening vision, begins a long discourse that continues to the end of chapter three (1:17b–3:20). This figure identifies himself as Jesus in verse 18, not by name but with the words, "I died, and behold I am alive forever and ever." Only near the end of the book, at 22:16, does this narrator say, "I, Jesus."

Of course, it is arguable that "John" is the true narrator all along because he quotes what Jesus said. But this is difficult to maintain because a number of voices other than John's break into the story line from time to time, sometimes at John's bidding and sometimes not. Who is the narrator, for example, in 1:1–3, where the letter from John has not formally begun and where God, Jesus, and John are all referred to in the third person? Is this someone other than John, and if so, isn't this person also in some sense the narrator of the rest of the book? Who is the narrator in 1:7–8, between John's epistolary introduction (vv. 4–6) and the beginning of his personal narrative (vv. 9–20)? Questions of this sort can be raised throughout the book; at the end, in 22:6–21, they become unavoidable.

It is probably better to acknowledge a plurality of narrators than to assign this role to John alone, or to argue that the (unknown) narrator of 1:1–3 is actually the narrator of the whole, or to contend that Jesus is the real narrator because the book claims to be a "revelation of Jesus Christ" (1:1). In a work consisting of a series of things seen and heard, it is more appropriate to speak of a number of *narrative voices* than of a single narrator.

Much has been written in connection with other New Testament books (especially the Gospel of John) about *narrative asides*, or brief explanatory intrusions by a narrator into the story line.[1] In the Revelation many such intrusions, introduced in a variety of ways, represent, so it seems, a variety of narrative voices.[2] As in more conventional narratives, such as the Gospels, the purpose of these intrusions is to explain to the reader what is going on. Sometimes they explain to John himself the significance of things he has just seen. A distinctive feature of a prophetic book such as Revelation is that John also is a kind of reader. He is trying to "read" his own visions, just as we are reading what he writes. John does not always understand everything he sees—at least he makes us believe this is the case—and some things must be explained to him, usually by an angel.

## The Importance of 1:19–20

The first such explanation of something John has seen comes in 1:20, where Jesus explains to John the "mystery" of the seven stars and the seven lampstands of verses 12 and 16. This is immediately preceded by a pronouncement of Jesus that is often regarded by students as a key to the structure of the entire book: γράψον οὖν ἃ εἶδες καὶ ἃ εἰσὶν καὶ ἃ μέλλει γενέσθαι μετὰ ταῦτα, *grapson oun ha eides kai ha eisin kai ha mellei genesthai meta tauta* (1:19). This sentence is commonly translated, "Write, therefore, the things you have seen and the things that are and the things that are going to happen afterward." It is commonly argued that "the things you have seen" comprise chapter 1, "the things that are," chapters 2–3, and "the things that are going to happen afterward," chapters 4–22.[3] More cautiously, some have suggested that "the things you have seen" actu-

---

1. On the Gospel of John see R. Alan Culpepper, *Anatomy of the Fourth Gospel: A Study in Literary Design* (Philadelphia: Fortress, 1983).

2. Much of the following discussion can be found in more detail in my article, "Revelation 1.19 and the Narrative Voices of the Apocalypse," *New Testament Studies* 37.4 (1991): 604–20.

3. For example, Henry B. Swete, *The Apocalypse of St. John* (London: Macmillan, 1922), 21; R. H. Charles, *The Revelation of St. John*, 2 vols., International Critical Commentary (Edinburgh: T. and T. Clark, 1920), 1.33.

ally consist of the entire book,[4] which is composed of two kinds of revelation: deeper insights into the present (including, though not limited to, chapters 1–3), and predictions of the future (including, though not limited to, chapters 4–22).[5]

A third way of reading 1:19 was common in the nineteenth century but is rarely encountered today: "Write, therefore the things you have seen, *and what they are,* and [consequently] the things that are going to happen afterward."[6] The difference between this interpretation and the other two is that the second term in the series, ἃ εἰσίν (*ha eisin*), is understood not as "the things that are" (emphasizing present time), but as "what they are" (emphasizing what the visions mean, or what they are about). The older commentators who held this view pointed to the accompanying explanation by the risen Jesus of "the mystery" (τὸ μυστήριον, *to mystērion*) of two details in the vision John had just seen (1:20): "The mystery of the seven stars *which you saw* [οὓς εἶδες, *hous eides*] in my right hand, and the seven golden lampstands: the seven stars *are* [εἰσιν] angels of the seven churches, and the seven lampstands *are* [εἰσιν] seven churches." The linking of οὓς εἶδες ("which you saw") with "are" (εἰσιν) recalls the first two terms of the formula in verse 19, ἃ εἶδες ("the things you have seen") and ἃ εἰσίν, supporting the translation of the latter as "what they are," or "what they mean." Εἰσίν is repeated here twice in connection with Jesus' authoritative explana-

---

4. The meaning would be, "the things you will have seen by the time you get around to writing them down." On this understanding, εἶδες corresponds to the ὅσα εἶδεν, "whatever things he saw," in 1:2; see also v. 11, "what you see [ὃ βλέπεις] write in a book."

5. This has become the most widely-held view today; see Isbon T. Beckwith, *The Apocalypse of John* (New York: Macmillan, 1919), 443; George R. Beasley-Murray, *The Book of Revelation*, New Century Bible (London: Oliphants, 1974), 68; G. B. Caird, *The Revelation of St. John the Divine*, Harper's New Testament Commentaries (New York: Harper and Row, 1966), 26, and Robert H. Mounce, *The Book of Revelation*, New International Commentary on the New Testament (Grand Rapids: Eerdmans, 1977), 82.

6. For example, Moses Stuart, *A Commentary on the Apocalypse* (Andover: Allen, Morrill, and Wardwell, 1845), 2.54; also Joseph A. Seiss, *The Apocalypse: Lectures on the Book of Revelation* (Grand Rapids: Zondervan, n.d.), 50. For the most part, the nineteenth century interpreters who defended this view seem to have confined the "the things you have seen" to the opening vision in 1:9–16, and "what they are" to the interpretation of that vision in v. 20 (perhaps including chaps. 2–3 as well). Only "the things that are going to happen afterward" were understood to refer to material found in the rest of the book.

tion of things John has just seen—that is, according to many nineteenth century interpreters his introductory vision of Jesus among the lampstands.

## John's Narrative Voice

If ἃ εἶδες ("the things you have seen") is understood to refer more broadly to the entire series of visions comprising the Revelation, the scope of this third interpretation is correspondingly widened. The student who looks for a pattern of things "seen" followed by an explanation of what they "are" will not be disappointed, for such a pattern occurs repeatedly. For example, John's vision of heaven in chapter 4, introduced by εἶδον ("I saw") in 4:1, includes "seven torches of fire burning before the throne, *which are* [ἅ εἰσιν] the seven spirits of God" (4:5). In chapter 5 he states, "And I saw [εἶδον]. . . . a Lamb standing as one slain, having seven heads and seven eyes, *which are* [οἵ εἰσιν] the seven spirits of God" (5:6). When the Lamb took the seven–sealed scroll, the four living creatures and twenty-four elders fell down before him, "each having a harp and golden bowls full of incense, *which are* [αἵ εἰσιν] the prayers of the saints" (5:8).

At the beginning of chapter 14, John says, "And I saw [εἶδον], and behold, the Lamb standing on Mount Zion, and with him 144,000, having his name and his Father's name written on their foreheads" (14:1). Later he describes these "144,000 who are redeemed from the earth" (v. 3) in the following way: "*These are* [οὗτοί εἰσιν, *houtoi eisin*] the ones who have not defiled themselves with women, for they *are* virgins" (14:4a). Then he adds, "*These* [οὗτοι] are the ones who have followed the Lamb wherever he went. *These* [οὗτοι] have been redeemed from humanity as first-fruits for God and the Lamb, and in their mouth was found no lie, for they *are* [εἰσιν] blameless" (14:4b–5).

In all these passages there is a distinction between things that John presumably could see in his visions, and things he could not actually see but about which he had some kind of higher knowledge, so that he could identify or explain them to his readers. For example, he "saw" (εἶδον) seven torches of fire (4:5) and the seven eyes of the Lamb (5:6), but he somehow knew that both represented "the seven spirits of God." He "saw" (εἶδον) the 144,000 (14:1), but it is hard to imagine how he could have actually seen their purity or virginity, or the fact that they had been redeemed and had "followed the Lamb wherever he went." Because he is a prophet as well as a seer, John is granted divine insight into the meaning of certain of his visions.

## Further Examples

In chapter 12, two signs in the sky "appeared" (ὤφθη, ōphthē) to John: a pregnant woman and a dragon waiting to devour the woman's child as soon as it is born (vv. 1–4). In 12:5 (although εἶδον is not used) John is understood to have seen the child's birth (v. 5a) and the taking of the child up to heaven to escape the dragon (v. 5c), but the fact that the child was "going to shepherd all the nations with a rod or iron" (v. 5b) is something John could not have seen. The child is identified here not by who he is ("This is Jesus," or "This is the Messiah"), but by what he is going to do. In the language of 1:19, we can say that the explanation comes not as "what these things are" (as in the examples from chapters 4, 5, and 14), but as "what is going to happen afterward." Yet the principle is the same. In 12:7–9, similarly, John saw the Dragon thrown out of heaven, but that the Dragon is to be identified as "the ancient serpent, who is called the Devil, and Satan, who deceives the whole world" (v. 9) is not part of the actual vision. It is something he already knows, perhaps as a prophet, and consequently is able to explain to the reader (see 20:2). To use the language of literary criticism, John often presents himself as a *reliable narrator*. He tells us that the "fine linen" worn by the bride of the Lamb is "the righteousness of the saints" (19:8b), thereby implying that the bride represents "the saints" (believers). He tells us that "the testimony of Jesus is the spirit of prophecy" (19:10), and that the "second death" is the "lake of fire" (20:14b). Sometimes such explanations will clarify things for the student and sometimes not, but those working on a text in Revelation can ill afford to neglect them. To some degree, at least, the Book of Revelation is self-interpreting.

## Other Voices

John himself is not always the reliable narrator. In chapter 7, for example, he says that "I saw [εἶδον], and behold, a great multitude that no one could number" (7:9). The multitude is from every nation on earth, standing before the throne of God, clothed in white, holding palm branches and ascribing salvation to God and the Lamb. This time John does not understand what he has seen. One of the twenty-four elders asks him, "Who are these, and where have they come from?" (v. 13).[7] When John disclaims all knowledge of the answer, the elder provides the correct interpretation: *"These are* [οὗτοι εἰσιν] the ones coming out of the great persecution; they have washed their robes and made them white in the blood of the Lamb. That is why they *are* [εἰσιν] before the throne of God, and are serving him day and night in his sanctuary" (vv. 14b–15a). The introductory εἶδον ("I saw") followed by the explanatory εἰσιν ("they are") exhibits again the pattern of "the things you have seen, and what they are," introduced in 1:19.

At this point the tense shifts from present to future; the elder, functioning as the "reliable narrator," continues his explanation of the unnumbered multitude from "what they are" to "what is going to happen afterward": "The One sitting on the throne *will* spread his tent over them. They *will* not be hungry any more, nor *will* they be thirsty any more, nor *will* the sun strike them, nor any scorching heat. For the Lamb in the middle of the throne *will* shepherd them and *will* lead them to springs of life-giving water. And God *will* wipe away every tear from their eyes" (7:15b–17). The elder's long identification of the unnumbered multitude leads into the fullest description of the final salvation of believers to be found prior to chapters 21–22.

An even more elaborate example of someone other than John taking on the role of reliable narrator is the interpretation in chapter 17 of the prostitute seated on the scarlet beast that had seven heads

---

7. We would have expected John to ask the question, but he never asks questions anywhere in the book, probably in agreement with an early Chistian notion that prophetic revelation was not to be solicited by questions, but given only at the initiative of God, Christ, or the Spirit (see *Shepherd of Hermas, Mandates* 11.2–6, and in the New Testament itself, John 16:23, 26, 30).

and ten horns. This vision, like the vision of the Risen Jesus in chapter 1, is called a "mystery" (17:5, 7; cf. 1:20), and just as in chapter 1 the mystery is explained to John in some detail. When John "saw" (εἶδον) the prostitute seated on the Beast, he was "greatly astonished" (v. 6). He was then told by the angel who had shown it to him ("one of the seven angels who had the seven bowls," v. 1), "Why are you astonished? I will tell you the mystery [τὸ μυστήριον] of the woman and the Beast that carries her who has the seven heads and the ten horns" (17:7; compare 1:20). Just as in chapter 7, John does not ask for the interpretation; the angel volunteers it (see footnote 7).

The rest of chapter 17 is the unveiling of the "mystery." Strictly speaking, John is still the narrator (see v. 15, "and he said to me"), but he speaks from a limited perspective. He merely reports what the angel has told him. The reliable narrator is the angel, who knows and is able to explain what even the smallest details in the vision mean. The angel refers repeatedly to that "which you saw" (εἶδες, vv. 8, 12, 15, 16, 18), and goes on to explain to John what it "is" (ἔστιν, vv. 11, 18), or what certain details "are" (εἰσιν, vv. 9, 12, 15). Again it is the pattern set forth in 1:19, "the things you have seen, and what they are," that governs the narrative interpretation of John's vision.

The angel begins with the Beast (v. 8) but is unwilling to say that the Beast "is" (ἔστιν), even in the rather neutral sense that the work of interpretation requires. Only God "is," in the sense that God is self-existent and eternal. Only God is ὁ ὤν ("the One who is," 1:4, 8; 4:8; 11:17; 16:5). So the identification of the Beast dissolves into a riddle, which is at the same time a parody of John's identification of God. If God is the One who "was, and is, and is to come" (4:8), the Beast is the one who "was, and *is not* [οὐκ ἔστιν, *ouk estin*], and is to ascend from the abyss and go to destruction," or more simply: "was, and is not, and will be" (v. 8).[8] The riddle is elaborated in verses 9–11, where the angel tells John that the seven heads of the Beast *"are* [εἰσιν] seven kings, five of whom have fallen, *one is* [ὁ εἷς ἔστιν], the other has not yet come, and when he comes he must

---

8. John's uses of "are not" (οὐκ εἰσίν) in the messages of chapters 2–3 to refer to people who claim to be something they are not, whether apostles (2:2) or Jews (2:9; 3:9). Throughout the book, John is vitally interested in the distinction between that which is true and that which is based on lies (see pp. 42–43).

remain only a little while. As for the Beast that was, and *is not* [οὐκ ἔστιν], he *is* an eighth [ὄγδοός ἐστιν, *ogdoos estin*], and [yet] *is* [ἔστιν] of the seven, and goes to destruction." For most modern readers the angel's explanation raises more questions than it answers, yet the focus of interest on what things "are" (in the sense of what they mean) and on "what is going to happen afterward" (in this case the coming and final destruction of the Beast) is maintained consistently.

The rest of the reliable narrator's identifications in this chapter are more straightforward. The angel calls for "a mind having wisdom" (v. 9a), and tells John that the Beast's seven heads "*are* [εἰσιν] seven hills where the woman is seated on them; and they *are* [εἰσιν] seven kings" (v. 9b).[9] In John's visionary world it does not matter if one image has two meanings, any more than it matters if two different images have the same meaning.[10] Neither explanation excludes the other. The "seven hills" suggest Rome even today,[11] but for the moment the angel is more interested in the seven kings viewed as a series (see pp. 44–46), and in reiterating the point made in verse 8 that the Beast, in his final manifestation, "has not yet come" (v. 10) and that when he comes his destruction is assured (v. 11).

The solution to the "mystery" continues in verses 12–18. The angel tells John that "the ten horns *which you saw* [ἃ εἶδες] *are* [εἰσιν] ten kings." Again there is a signal that these kings are future: they have "not yet received [οὔπω ἔλαβον, *oupō elabon*] dominion, but they receive authority as kings for one hour with the Beast. *These* have one mind, and give their power and their authority to the Beast. *These* will make war with the Lamb, and the Lamb will conquer them" (vv. 12–14a). As in such passages as 7:14–17 and 11:3–13, there is a shift from present tense to future, and it is likely here (as in 11:3–13) that even the present tenses have a future meaning.[12] Once again the "reliable narrator" moves on from what certain

---

9. The translation is literal. The redundant construction illustrates again the influence of Hebrew on John's grammar (see chapter 5).

10. For the latter, see 4:5 and 5:6, where either seven torches of fire or the seven eyes of the Lamb can represent the seven spirits of God; also 11:4, where God's two witnesses are represented both as two olive trees and two lampstands.

11. For ancient references to Rome being built on seven hills (Virgil, Ovid, Martial, Cicero) see Swete, *Apocalypse*, 220.

12. See the discussion of 11:1–13 on p. 88.

things "are" to "what is going to happen afterward." The interest in
the ten kings is interrupted briefly by the angel's statement that "the
waters *which you saw* [ἃ εἶδες], where the prostitute is seated, *are*
[εἰσιν] peoples and multitudes and nations and languages" (v.
15)—possibly with the implication that these are the peoples and
nations to be ruled by the ten kings.

At any rate, the story of "the ten horns that you saw" resumes
with the prediction that they (and the Beast with them) will turn
against the prostitute and destroy her (v. 16). All of this takes place
by the sovereign direction of God "until the words of God are
brought to completion" (v. 17). Finally the prostitute herself is identified: "And the woman *whom you saw* [ἣν εἶδες] *is* [ἔστιν] the great
city that has dominion over the kings of the earth" (v. 18). If the
"seven hills" of verse 9 suggested that the prostitute named "Babylon" (v. 5) represented the city of Rome, this conclusion to the "mystery" makes the identification all but unmistakable. It is difficult to
imagine how any city but Rome could have been viewed in the late
first century A.D. as having "dominion over the kings of the earth."
The identification of the prostitute as Rome in chapter 17 has
become, in the history of interpretation, every bit as much a fixed
point of reference for students of this book as the identification of
the Dragon as Satan in chapter 12.

## A Hermeneutic of Suspicion?

Normally the student will want to take advantage of these fixed
reference points in interpreting the Revelation, whether John himself provides them as reliable narrator or whether they are attributed to a supernatural being, such as Jesus, an elder, or an angel.

Some people, however, are naturally suspicious, and there is in
recent literary criticism a movement known as *deconstruction* which
attempts to subvert the very author or text it is studying. In biblical
criticism the term *hermeneutic of suspicion* is sometimes used by
those who come to the Bible from certain ideological perspectives
that see themselves excluded from biblical scholarship or even from
the world of the Bible itself (for example, feminist or Third World
liberationist theologies). Such a hermeneutic does not always trust
the biblical author's intent. It may go so far as to take up the cause

of the biblical author's opponents, or it may content itself with suggesting that the issues were not quite so one-sided as the biblical text would have us believe.[13] In a broader sense, however, anyone who tries to square the ancient biblical text with modern values at times will come to practice a hermeneutic of suspicion.[14]

In the past, those who have taken this route in connection with the Book of Revelation usually have done so by attributing certain interpretations built into John's visions to sources or redactors that somehow did not represent the mind of the author. Either the author used sources with which he was not fully in agreement, or else one or more redactors changed the author's intended meaning. This tendency is evident in the commentary of R. H. Charles, and in the work of a number of other scholars, especially on Revelation 17. More recent trends in literary criticism make it possible to achieve a comparable result, even while maintaining a kind of literary unity of the book, simply by regarding the narrator as unreliable. But if the narrator, whether John or an angel or the Jesus of John's visions, is an "unreliable narrator," where does that leave us? In the words of Peter in John 6:68, "To whom shall we go?"

An example may be useful. Are we really so sure that the woman on the scarlet Beast in chapter 17 is, as the narrator seems to tell us, Rome? Another, very different, woman was introduced at the beginning of chapter 12. This woman gave birth to a Child-Messiah (12:5), and was pursued by the great Dragon into a place prepared for her in the desert, where she was protected for 1260 days (12:6), or for "a time, times, and half a time" (12:14). This woman is not identified by John or any other narrator, and consequently her identity is debated. Clearly, however, she is presented in a positive light as antagonist and potential victim of the evil Dragon. Because the other symbolic women in Revelation are cities (the Prostitute in 17:18, and the Bride in 21:9–10), it is natural to identify this woman

---

13. An example of the latter tendency is the work of Leonard Thompson (*The Book of Revelation: Apocalypse and Empire* [New York: Oxford University Press, 1990], esp. chaps. 11–12), who suggests that in the seven churches of Asia, John may have been the extremist while the "Nicolaitans," who advocated compromise with the existing Roman culture, were the moderates.

14. This happens even—perhaps especially—from the pulpit, and most often in connection with "hard sayings" of Jesus such as "love your enemies," or "turn the other cheek," or "sell all you have and give to the poor."

too as a city. The most common interpretation is that she is Jerusalem or Zion, "mother" of all the people of God—the old Jerusalem, perhaps, in distinction from the new Jerusalem of chapter 21.

In any event, this "good" woman disappears from view at the end of chapter 12. We leave her safe in the desert (εἰς τὴν ἔρημον, *eis tēn erēmon* 12:14; compare 12:6). As for the "evil" woman, the prostitute on the scarlet Beast in chapter 17, John's first glimpse of her is in the desert as well (εἰς ἔρημον, 17:3). A "deconstructionist" reading of the text could infer that the "good" woman had made her peace with the forces of evil and now stood defiantly on the other side! In other words, "Babylon," the prostitute of chapter 17, is not Rome but Jerusalem![15] Such a view could appeal for support to 11:8, where the bodies of the two witnesses lie in the streets of "the great city, which is called spiritually Sodom and Egypt, where their Lord also was crucified." Here the term "great city," which elsewhere refers to "Babylon" (16:19; 17:18; 18:10, 16, 19; see also 14:8; 17:5; 18:2) seems to refer to Jerusalem, for it was undeniably in Jerusalem and not in Rome that Jesus was crucified. Is it possible that "Jerusalem" wears two different faces in the Revelation?

The purpose of this example is not to suggest that those who argue in this way are correct—I, for one, do not think they are—but simply to underscore the ambiguity of much of the symbolism in Revelation. If the "reliable narrator" points us in one specific direction, we may well conclude that this identification is a legitimate reading—probably the best reading—of the text. But must we insist that it is the *only* possible reading? Even the reliable narrator sometimes points us to two legitimate interpretations at once (for example, the seven heads of the Beast as seven hills and as seven kings). It is therefore wise not to be limited by the "built-in" interpretations found in the text, however much we may benefit from them, but to allow the richness of the book's symbolism to raise questions that even a reliable narrator may not have been conclusively answered.

---

15. See the argument of Josephine Massyngberde Ford, *Revelation*, Anchor Bible 38 (Garden City, N.Y.: Doubleday, 1975), 282–86, who, however, is not "deconstructing" anything, but believes that this is actually what the angel's words mean.

# 7

# Tradition History: Images Transformed

The uniqueness of the Book of Revelation in the New Testament rests on a kind of paradox: While it makes far greater use of the Hebrew Bible or Old Testament[1] than any other New Testament writing, the Old Testament is never actually quoted. There are no claims that specific biblical texts are "fulfilled" in events recorded here, in the sense that Matthew points to fulfilled prophecies in Jesus' life. Instead, Revelation draws on the imagery and language of the Old Testament on almost every line. This book only can be interpreted by keeping one eye on the Old Testament and asking again and again how John uses the ancient text.

In this respect the Revelation provides an excellent example—perhaps the best New Testament example—of a phenomenon known in literary criticism as *intertextuality*. Recognizing intertextuality means reading all texts in relationship to earlier texts. Nothing is written in a vacuum; in computer terminology, we might say that

---

1. The term *Old Testament* can be used when the student is discussing the Christian use of the Hebrew Bible, whether by New Testament writers or Christians of later generations. When the student is discussing the Hebrew Bible in and of itself, it is more appropriate to call it either the Hebrew Bible, the Jewish Bible, or (unless there is danger of confusion with the whole Christian Bible) simply Scripture, the Scriptures, or the Bible. This body of literature, after all, belonged first to the Jews, and from a Jewish perspective it is emphatically *not* the "Old" Testament.

all texts update an existing file.[2] Some interrelated texts form net-
works known as *genres* (see pp. 21-27).[3]

Because there are few epistles but many prophecies in the
Hebrew Bible it is not surprising that the Revelation, written by one
who considered himself a prophet, draws repeatedly on the language and imagery of the Hebrew prophets. But John does not limit
himself to the prophets; he also makes generous use of the Psalms
and a number of biblical narratives. His network is far larger than
any one genre, nor is it limited to the Old Testament. John also uses
sayings of Jesus similar to those found in the Gospels and a variety
of popular Jewish and Hellenistic traditions, to an extent difficult to
determine.

Tradition history or tradition analysis,[4] therefore, is a very different enterprise in the Book of Revelation than in the Synoptic
Gospels. Older works approached it as if it were much the same, a
matter of sources and various redactors. The classic example is the
1920 commentary of R. H. Charles. More recent scholarship has
recognized that, for the most part, the intertextuality of Revelation
is not attributable to written sources,[5] but to the book's intrinsic
literary character. The title of Austin Farrer's 1949 work is sugges-
tive: "A Rebirth of Images."[6] G. B. Caird acknowledged Farrer as
the one "who first opened my eyes to John's use of the imagination

---

2. Another useful metaphor is that of the *palimpsest*, a manuscript written (for
reasons of economy) over an older manuscript that had been partially erased.

3. A study of interrelated texts and genres is that of Gregory Linton, "Overrun-
ning the Boundaries: Intertextuality and the Problem of the Genre of the Revelation
of John" (paper read at the 1990 meeting of the Society of Biblical Literature).

4. Scot McKnight, *Interpreting the Synoptic Gospels* (Grand Rapids: Baker, 1988);
see esp. chaps. 6–8 on the historical criticism, form criticism, and redaction criticism
of the Synoptic Gospels.

5. The possibility of sources and redaction is still raised in certain passages (for
example, the vision of the 144,000 in Revelation 7, the account of the two witnesses
in chap. 11, the double account of the woman and the Dragon in 12:1–6 and 12:7–18,
and the series of seven kings in 17:9b–10), and on a much larger scale by isolated
commentators, for example, Josephine Massyngberde Ford, *Revelation*, Anchor
Bible 38 (New York: Doubleday, 1975).

6. The full reference is *A Rebirth of Images: The Making of St John's Apocalypse*
(Westminster: Dacre, 1949; repr. ed. Boston: Beacon, 1963). For a more disciplined
development of Farrer's approach, see his commentary, *The Revelation of St. John the
Divine* (Oxford: Clarendon, 1964).

and taught me to see in him both an exegete and a supreme literary artist."[7]

The notion of John as "exegete" is at first puzzling. An exegete interprets, and the student will be surprised to learn that John was doing the same thing the student now does. Yet we saw in the preceding chapter how John (or someone greater than he) interpreted his visions within the text of the Revelation itself. In this chapter we will see how John exegetes, or interprets, ancient and not-so-ancient texts and traditions, not so much as a scholar sifts through old manuscripts but as an actor interprets Shakespeare by bringing a play to life for a new generation in a new setting. Just as we do not need Shakespeare's text—much less Shakespeare's sources—in front of us in order to enjoy the play, so we do not have to grasp all the Old Testament allusions in Revelation to feel the wonder and power of the book's imagery. John's language takes on a life of its own, for it is at once the interpretation of something old and the creation of something new. This is the rebirth or transformation of which Farrer, Caird, and others have spoken, and it is fully appreciated only through examples.

## John's First Vision

The student senses the overwhelming power of the sights and sounds of John's initial experience on Patmos recounted in 1:9–20, but for the meaning must rely on an interpretation woven into the text. The figure "like a son of man," whose voice is heard in verses 10–11, and who makes himself visible in verses 12–16, takes on the role of reliable narrator, identifying himself implicitly as Jesus by referring to Jesus' resurrection (vv. 17b–18; see p. 96). Most students, if they have read the Book of Revelation before, know the identification. Therefore, although they feel the power of verses 12–16, they are unable to share or fully understand the prophet's terror ("I fell at his feet like a dead man," v. 17a). They can only appreciate this terror if they are somehow able to read the account as if for the first time. This perspective is one of the goals of exegesis.

---

7. G. B. Caird, *A Commentary on the Revelation of St. John the Divine*, Harper's New Testament Commentaries (New York: Harper and Row, 1966), v.

Without the self-identification in verses 17b–18, the figure "like a son of man" would be simply an angel like the angels who appeared to many of the heroes and prophets in the Hebrew Bible. Not even the phrase, "like a son of man," in Revelation 1:13 necessarily connects him with Jesus, despite Jesus' self-designation as "*the* Son of Man," for the phrase merely indicates that the figure was human in form and appearance, as are most angels.[8]

The student should learn to ask where in the Bible we have seen such a figure before. Which biblical passage establishes the point of departure or springboard for John's description? This question can be asked of almost every text in the Revelation. Sometimes there is one biblical passage, sometimes more than one, but it is useful to choose one as a starting point and try to see what light the use of this text sheds on the new text John has written in Revelation. In the process other passages, both biblical and post-biblical, will come into the picture, and the student will begin to see how intertextuality becomes a tool in exegesis.

In this instance students will discover that the figure who appears to John reminds one of the angel who confronted Daniel in Daniel 10:4–6. Most will notice this, not because of prior knowledge of Daniel, but by paying close attention to the marginal references in N[26]. Daniel's vision also has a precise geographical location "on the bank of the great river, the Tigris" (10:4, compare with Rev. 1:9, "on the island called Patmos"). Daniel saw "a *man, clothed* in linen, his loins *girded* with the finest gold and his body as chrysolite, his face as lightning, *his eyes* as torches of fire, his arms and *feet* as burnished *bronze*, and *his voice* as *the voice* of a multitude" (10:5–6). Although the vocabulary differs in Revelation, the overall effect is much the same. John saw "someone like a son of *man, clothed* down to his feet and *girded* around the chest with a *gold* belt. His head and the hairs [of it] were white as wool, and *his eyes* as a blaze of fire, and his *feet* like *fine bronze* as [if] fired in the furnace, and *his voice* as the *voice* of many waters, and having in his right hand seven stars, and coming out of his mouth a sharp two edged sword, and his appearance shines like the sun in its power" (1:13–16). The italicized words

---

8. Ibid., 25. Caird's use of the term *Son of Man* for this figure as if that were his title is misleading, for it implies that John immediately recognized him as Jesus, the "Son of man" of the Gospels.

will show in a general way where the vocabularies of the two passages correspond.

This kind of information often becomes useful in comparing texts in the Revelation with texts in the Hebrew Bible or Greek Old Testament. Students will want to use the Hebrew text or a fairly literal English translation such as the RSV, and the Greek Old Testament.[9] The text of Daniel is complicated by the existence of two Greek translations, the LXX and the version of Theodotion; both, however, are found in standard editions of the LXX.[10] The Greek Bible is important because it permits a word-by-word comparison with the text of Revelation, and provides evidence of how Hebrew words were understood and translated in the Hellenistic world in which the Book of Revelation was written.

In the first vision, the parallels extend beyond Daniel 10:4–6; there are other parallels within Daniel 10. Daniel by the Tigris, like John on Patmos, is overwhelmed with fear and helplessness (10:8–9, 15–17; compare Rev. 1:17a). Daniel, like John, is touched by the figure before him (10:10, 18), and is told, "Do not be afraid" (μὴ φοβοῦ, mē phobou, 10:19; compare Rev. 1:17b). Daniel's angel is called "a certain man" (Theodotion: ἀνὴρ εἷς, anēr heis; LXX: ἄνθρωπος εἷς, anthrōpos heis, 10:5), or "as the sight of a man" (ὡς ὅρασις ἀνθρώπου, hōs horasis anthrōpou, 10:18), while John sees one "like a son of man" (ὅμοιον υἱὸν ἀνθρώπου, homoion huion anthrōpou, 1:13).

At this point, the marginal notes in N[26] are again helpful. Another text from Daniel is mentioned in which someone "as a son of man" (ὡς υἱὸς ἀνθρώπου, hōs huios anthrōpou) was seen coming either "on" (LXX) or "with" (Theodotion) the "clouds of heaven" (Dan. 7:13). This text, which influenced the presentation of Jesus as "Son of Man" in the Gospels, is important here as well, even though its vocabulary does not match exactly that of Revelation 1:13. Daniel 7:13 provides one detail regarding John's vision in Revelation 1 that

---

9. The Greek Old Testament is the Septuagint, hereafter referred to by its standard abbreviation, the LXX (a Roman numeral referring to the "seventy" scholars said to have prepared the translation). For the LXX text students should use A. Rahlfs' edition (Stuttgart: 1965).

10. Students who have difficulty with the Greek of the Septuagint should consult the English translation of it by L. C. L. Brenton, *The Septuagint Version in English*, 2 vols. (London: Bagster, 1844; repr. ed., Peabody, Mass.: Hendrickson); based on Codex Vaticanus.

was not noticeably influenced by the vision of Daniel 10: "His *head and the hairs [of it]* were *white as wool,* and his eyes *as a blaze of fire*" (1:14). This language too is from Daniel 7, but not from the description of the one who came "as a son of man." It recalls instead the description of "the Ancient of Days" in Daniel 7:9, who had "clothing as *white* as snow, and *the hair of his head as white as wool,* and his throne *as a blaze of fire*" (italics highlight parallels). The figure in John's vision combines in itself the features of the one "as a son of man" (both in Daniel 7 and 10) with the features of the "Ancient of Days" in Daniel 7.

Another reference in the N[26] margin points the student to the introductory vision of Ezekiel (Ezek. 1:26), where, over a shining expanse, "on what looked like a throne, of what looked like sapphire," Ezekiel saw "what looked like the form of a man above it" (LXX: ὁμοίωμα ὡς εἶδος ἀνθρώπου ἄνωθεν, *homoiōma hōs eidos anthrōpou anōthen*).[11] Another points to Ezekiel 9:2, 3, 11 (LXX), where Ezekiel speaks of "a man *clothed down to his feet,* and a sapphire *belt* around his waist" (italics indicate parallels with Rev. 1:13).[12]

These are some of the texts with which John interacts in Revelation 1:12–16. Caird rightly warns us that "to compile such a catalogue is to unweave the rainbow. John uses his allusions not as a code in which each symbol requires separate and exact translation, but rather for their evocative and emotive power."[13] The student's purpose in unweaving this particular rainbow is not to spoil its dramatic effect, but to appreciate that this first vision of John is not intrinsically christological, any more than the corresponding visions of Daniel or Ezekiel were christological. The unweaving helps us to see the vision with John, as if for the first time and from a kind of Old Testament perspective. John does not know he has seen Jesus until the figure so identifies himself. What he has seen,

---

11. Notice the apocalyptic reserve in the language of all three prophets, in which the visionary stops short of saying outright that he saw anything positively identifiable, only that he saw "what looked like" the object in question.

12. Caird (*Commentary,* 25) mentions as well the "belt" or "girdle," and the "robe down to the feet" (ποδήρη, *podērē*) worn by the Jewish high priest (Exod. 28:4; 39:29), but these priestly features more likely influenced Ezekiel than the Book of Revelation directly.

13. Ibid.

and we have seen with him, is an angel resplendent with the majesty—even the white hair—of the eternal God, known to Daniel as the "Ancient of Days." This particular angel, of course, turns out to be Jesus, but from John's perspective this does not make him any less an angel.[14] Only the "sharp two edged sword" coming out of the angel's mouth depends for its meaning on the subsequent identification of the angel as Jesus (see 2:12; 19:15, 21; Heb. 4:12).

The student will have to ask at some point how conclusive this angel's self-identification is for later visions in the Book of Revelation. When we meet another angel "like a son of man" (ὅμοιον υἱὸν ἀνθρώπου) seated on a white cloud in 14:14, are we to conclude that this too is Jesus? Our reliable narrator does not help us out this time, and it is wise not to read into the text an identification where none is given. The angel in chapter 14 is merely one of a series of angels carrying out the judgment of God, and (in spite of familiar references to Jesus the Son of Man coming on, or with, the clouds)[15] the student is safer in leaving it at that. The angel "harvests the earth" (14:16), and another angel in the same series harvests the earth's vineyard, throwing the grapes into "the winepress of God's great wrath, and the winepress was trampled outside the city, and blood flowed from the winepress up to the horses' bridles for 1600 stadia" (14:19–20; see also Isa. 63:1–3). Not until five chapters later, when he refers again to the "winepress," does John introduce a rider on a white horse, called "Faithful and True" (19:11) and "the Word of God" (v. 13), who has the familiar "eyes as a blaze of fire" (v. 12) and the "sharp sword coming out of his mouth" (v. 15a). It is he (καὶ αὐτός, kai autos, v. 15b), says John, heaping up genitives for dramatic effect, who "tramples the winepress of the wine of the anger of the wrath of Almighty God." The rider has yet a third name written on his robe and on his thigh: "King of kings and Lord of lords" (v. 16).

---

14. See the second-century *Shepherd of Hermas* for the difficulty the reader has in determining whether the angel who appears repeatedly to the prophet Hermas as a shepherd is Jesus, or simply an angel.

15. See the New Testament references to Jesus coming "with the clouds" (Rev. 1:7), or as Son of Man either "in clouds" (Mark 13:26), or "in a cloud" (Luke 21:27), or "with the clouds of heaven" (Mark 14:62), or "on the clouds of heaven" (Matt. 24:30; 26:64).

revealed that the angels who carried out the judgments of chapter 14 were his agents and surrogates as well. In a sense, those who identify the angel of 14:14 or the angel of 14:19–20 as Jesus Christ are not wrong, only premature. As a rule the student should stay within the bounds of whatever specific vision is under discussion, and not go beyond what is apparent to John at that moment, or what is made explicit by a reliable narrator. Let angels be angels! My experience in the classroom has been that when I ask first year students who the figure in Rev. 1:12–16 is, many of them do not know until I explain it to them on the basis of verses 17b–18. I used to be impatient with them until I realized that without even trying they were approaching the text in exactly the right way. Sometimes we know too much to begin with to be good interpreters!

## The Throne Room and the Glassy Sea

John's second vision is a glimpse into heaven itself. He saw a throne with a rainbow like an emerald around it, and "someone seated" on the throne with an appearance like jasper and carnelian stone. Around it were twenty-four additional thrones with twenty-four elders seated on them. "Lightnings and voices and thunders" were coming from the throne, while in front of it were "seven torches of fire" and something "as a sea of glass, like crystal." "In the midst of the throne" and around it were "four living creatures full of eyes before and behind," one like a lion, one like an ox, one with a face like a human being, and one like a flying eagle (Rev. 4:2–7).

This time I will leave it to the student to trace the extent to which this is a rewriting or a transformation of more ancient visions. Probably the best starting point is the vision of Ezekiel (Ezek. 1:4–28) was of some significance for the interpretation of Revelation 1:12–16. There too the prophet was looking into heaven itself. The reader will find in Ezekiel's vision a throne (1:26), a figure surrounded by a rainbow (1:28), "fire flashing" (1:4), and in the midst of the fire "what looked like four living creatures" (1:5; see also Isa. 6:1–4). Transformation is evident, however, in the fact that for Ezekiel each of the living creatures had four faces on four sides (a human, a lion, an ox, and an eagle, 1:10), while for John each living creature had a different face.

Not every detail in John's vision comes from Ezekiel. The "light-nings and voices and thunders," for example, echo the language of the power of God displayed to Moses and the people on Mount Sinai (Exod. 19:16), while the twenty-four elders on their thrones who join the four living creatures in praising God (Rev. 4:4, 10) are difficult to explain as a rewriting of any specific text. There were of course elders in Israel. In Exodus, seventy of them went up Mount Sinai with Moses, Aaron, Nadab, and Abihu and "saw the God of Israel, and under his feet something like a pavement of sapphire, clear as the sky itself" (Exod. 24:1, 9–10). There were also "elders" in the Christian churches by John's time (see Acts 14:23; 20:17–35; 1 Pet. 5:1–4; Titus 1:5–6), and John would also have known that there were 24 orders of priests for ministering in the temple of Jerus-alem (1 Chron. 24:1–19). Quite possibly this aspect of John's vision grows out of an analogy between earthly and heavenly worship.

Another difficult detail is "the sea of glass, like crystal" (4:6). Its only possible reference point in Ezekiel 1 is the "expanse" (Hebrew: רָקִיעַ, *rāqîaʿ*; LXX: στερέωμα, *stereōma*) that the prophet saw above the four living creatures, "as the sight of crystal" (Ezek. 1:22). But Ezekiel neither calls it a sea nor mentions glass. Caird, without referring to Ezekiel, finds in this "sea of glass" the "one discordant note" in John's vision of heaven. By linking it with two other refer-ences in Revelation to the sea, he understands it as "the reservoir of evil out of which arises the monster" (13:1), and the one sphere of creation that does not appear in the new heaven and the new earth (21:1). "The *sea*," he says, "whether on earth or in heaven, belongs essentially to the old order, and within that order it stands for everything that is recalcitrant to the will of God."[16]

It is safe to say that the notion of a "reservoir of evil" in heaven will be a novel one to most students. Caird's striking suggestion provides a useful case study by which we can learn to test the validity of other people's theories and, more importantly, our own. The best way to test this particular theory is by a word study of *sea* (θάλασσα, *thalassa*) as it is used in the Revelation and, to a limited degree, elsewhere. Such a study will show that *sea* is used twenty-six times in the Revelation. Of these, nineteen refer to the sea from a neutral standpoint, as part of God's creation along with

---

16. Caird, *Commentary,* 65.

the earth, the sky, and the sources of fresh water (for example, 14:7). As such, the sea is subjected to God's judgments (8:8–9; 16:3), but no more so than the rest of the natural environment (8:7, 10–12; 16:1–2, 4–9). Three references specify the "sea of glass" in heaven (4:6 and two occurrences in 15:2). Only four of the twenty-six carry anything like the evil connotation which Caird finds so conspicuous: 13:1, which he mentions, along with a reference preceding it in 12:18, to the Dragon standing "on the sand of the sea"; 21:1, which he also mentions, and a reference in 20:13 to the sea, along with "death and Hades," as a realm of the dead. In addition, Caird claims the "sea of glass" in 15:2 as "the barrier which the redeemed must pass in a new Exodus, if they are to win access to the promised land."[17]

Caird's reading is the result of placing all his emphasis on the word *sea*, while ignoring the accompanying adjective *of glass* (ὑαλίνη, *hyalinē*) and the descriptive phrase *like crystal*. The latter, as we have seen, links John's "glassy sea" to his primary text, Ezekiel 1:22, and to Ezekiel's great "expanse" that was "as the sight of crystal." In John's vision of the new Jerusalem, the city's appearance is compared to "jasper stone shining like crystal" (κρυσταλλίζοντι, *krystallizonti*, 21:11). The reference to "glass" is picked up in the same vision, where the Holy City is said to be "pure gold, like pure glass" (ὅμοιον ὑάλῳ καθαρῷ, *homoion hyalō katharō*, 21:18), and the street of the city is said to be "pure gold, transparent as glass" (ὡς ὕαλος διαυγής, *hōs hyalos diaugēs*, 21:21). Although it is true that there is no sea in John's new creation, the distinctive quality of the "sea of glass, like crystal" pervades the city where the glory of God is forever displayed. Even more to the point, the city has "a river of water of life, bright as crystal (λαμπρὸν ὡς κρύσταλλον, *lampron hōs krystallon*), going out from the throne of God and the Lamb" (22:1). Unless John is being extremely subtle, the glassy, crystalline appearance of the sea in 4:6 is no aura of evil, but a signal that this detail, like everything else in the chapter, radiates the glory of God. Revelation 15:2 is no different, for its description of the sea of glass as "mixed with fire" is simply an effort to evoke together the "seven torches of fire" and the "sea of glass," both "before the throne of

---

17. Ibid.

God," from the earlier vision (4:5–6). Far from being a "barrier" to the people of God, it is a clear signal that their victory has been won.

Why then does John speak of a "sea" in 4:6 instead of a crystalline "expanse" (as does Ezek. 1:22) or a sapphire pavement (like Exod. 24:10)? Possibly he views the heavenly throne room as a kind of temple, and is thinking of the giant bronze laver, called a "sea," that stood in the temple at Jerusalem (1 Kings 7:23–26; also 2 Chron. 4:4–6). Caird argues that even in the temple the sea was "a cosmic symbol representing the primeval ocean of the creation myth"—a subtle interpretation which he admits was already missed by the chronicler![18] Alternatively, the sea may be intended to recall Genesis 1:7, where an "expanse" (Hebrew: רָקִיעַ; Greek: στερέωμα, as in Ezek. 1:22) separated the waters above from the waters below. The word *sea* in 4:6 may simply apply the term for the waters below (Gen. 1:10) to the waters above, the source of rain and life on the earth.

*Sea* in the rest of the Revelation (except for 15:2) is best understood simply as part of the natural environment. It takes on the grim connotations noticed by Caird only because (like Hades) it is a grave for the dead (20:13). To say there is "no more sea" (21:1) is merely another way of saying there is no more death (20:14; 21:4). Because the depths of the sea, like the depths of the earth, always have been a mystery and a source of terror, John can depict the Beast as rising either "out of the abyss" (11:7; 17:8) or "out of the sea" (13:1; compare Dan. 7:3). There is no more need to equate the sea on earth with the crystal sea in heaven than there is to connect the "many waters" where Babylon the prostitute was seated (17:1, 15) with the "sound of many waters" echoing several times in the book from heaven and heavenly beings (1:15; 14:2; 19:6; compare Ezek. 1:24). Caird's view is challenging and thought-provoking, but the student will do well to subject it to careful scrutiny.

## John's Call to Prophesy

If Revelation 1:9–20 is John's introductory vision and his call to write, and if chapters 4–5 record his first glimpse into heaven, then

---

18. Ibid.

10:1–13 is his call to *prophesy* in the classic sense of that word. Once again the biblical point of departure is Ezekiel. The interest in Ezekiel's prophetic call (Ezek. 2:8–3:7) is not surprising in view of the extensive use of that prophet's introductory vision (Ezek. 1:10, 22–28) in John's earlier visions. Ezekiel was told by "the appearance of the likeness of the glory of the Lord" (1:28) to "open your mouth and eat what I give you" (2:8b). Then he saw "a hand stretched out to me, and in it a scroll of a book [LXX: κεφαλὶς βιβλίου, *kephalis bibliou*]. And he unrolled it before me, and it was written on the front and back, and what was written on it was lament and mourning and woe" (2:9–10). Ezekiel is told again to "let your stomach eat, and fill your belly with this scroll [τῆς κεφαλίδος ταύτης, *tēs kephalidos tautēs*] I am giving you." When Ezekiel ate, "it was in my mouth sweet like honey" (3:3).

In Revelation, John is given a "little scroll" (βιβλαρίδιον, *biblaridion*, 10:2, 9, 10) or simply a "scroll" (βίβλιον, *biblion*, v. 8), not by an anonymous hand from God, but by "another strong angel coming down out of heaven, clothed with a cloud, and the rainbow at his head, and his face as the sun, and his feet as pillars of fire" (10:1). This angel "placed his right foot on the sea and the left [foot] on the earth, and cried out with a great voice, as a lion roars" (vv. 2–3a). The phrase, *strong angel*, recalls the "strong angel" of 5:2, who had also spoken with "a great voice" when he asked "Who is worthy to open the scroll [ανοῖξαι τὸ βίβλιον, *anoixai to biblion*] and to loose its seals?" It is not clear whether the word *another* (ἄλλον, *allon*) in 10:1 is used in reference to the previous "strong angel," implying that this is a *different* strong angel, or in reference to the six angels who blew the first six trumpets in chapters 8–9 ("And I saw another angel, a strong one"). In either case, the phrase recalls the beginning of chapter 5, for both strong angels are seen in connection with a scroll (βίβλιον) of some significance. Moreover, "the rainbow" (ἡ ἶρις, *hē iris*) at the angel's head in chapter 10 recalls, perhaps intentionally, the rainbow around the throne of God (4:3) in the setting of the scene for chapters 4–5.[19]

---

19. It is even possible that the definite article with "rainbow" in 10:1, which is grammatically unnecessary and omitted by some manuscripts (see N[26]), was used to call attention to the parallel with 4:3 ("the rainbow previously mentioned"). See p. 85.

John's horizons in Revelation 10 are different from Ezekiel's because they are set by internal factors in the Book of Revelation itself. Ezekiel could see that his scroll was "written on the front and back" because the scroll was unrolled before his eyes. He saw written there "lament and mourning and woe" (Ezek. 2:10). John somehow knew that the scroll he saw in chapter 5 was "written inside and on the back," even though it was unopened and sealed with seven seals! Evidently he knew this just as he knew what the eyes of the Lamb and the incense bowls held by the elders and living creatures meant (5:6, 8), because he was a reliable narrator (see pp. 99–100). On the other hand, when he sees the "open scroll" in 10:2, he sees no writing on it at all.

John has elaborated the simple account of Ezekiel eating the scroll and finding it sweet like honey in his mouth (Ezek. 3:3; compare Ps. 119:103) into a kind of chiasm (an a–b–b–a pattern). First the angel tells John, "Take and eat it,[20] and [a] *it will make your stomach bitter, but* [b] *in your mouth it will be sweet as honey*" (Rev. 10:9). Then when John took the scroll and ate it, his reaction is described in reverse order: "And I took the scroll from the angel's hand, and ate it, and it was [b] *in my mouth sweet as honey,* and when I ate it, [a] *my stomach was made bitter*" (v. 10). The effect of the chiasm is to place the emphasis on the bitterness in John's stomach,[21] which appears to be his equivalent to the "lament and mourning and woe" written on the scroll (Ezek. 2:10), as well as the bitterness and anger in Ezekiel's spirit when he went to the Jewish exiles (2:14). It is in the content of the scroll, John's prophecies to "peoples and nations and languages and many kings" (Rev. 10:13), that his stomach will turn bitter, for his prophecies to the nations will be prophecies of woe (the account of the two witnesses in 11:3–13, and the announcement of the "third woe" in 11:14).

Most of the imagery that does not come from Ezekiel is taken from other parts of the Revelation. John's transformations of the

---

20. The reference to "taking" as well as "eating" the scroll is not found in Ezekiel, and recalls the emphasis in Revelation 5 on the Lamb "taking" the scroll there in order to open its seals (5:7–9). The combination "take" and "eat" also may have evoked associations with the Lord's Supper in early Christianity (Matt. 26:26).

21. It is worth noting that Ezekiel, without speaking of bitterness in the stomach, does mention the stomach twice, redundantly and with two different words, in 3:3.

story of Ezekiel's call tend to suggest that the scroll of Revelation 10 may indeed be the scroll, now opened, of chapter 5, and that the rest of the book is the bittersweet transcribing of the scroll's contents (see the questions raised on pp. 60–61, about the structure of the book).[22] Students who have gotten this far in our discussion will have to test that theory for themselves, just as we tested Caird's theory.

## Revelation 12–13: Myth or Midrash?

The heart of the conflict dominating the latter half of the Revelation is found in chapters 12–13. Here, as elsewhere, John rewrites and transforms earlier texts and traditions. But what texts does he rewrite? More than one apparently. Caird finds an exposition of Psalm 2 in the setting of these chapters: in 11:15, "our Lord and his Christ" (see Ps. 2:2); 11:18, "the nations raged" (see Ps. 2:1); 12:5, the Child "who will shepherd the nations with a rod of iron" (see Ps. 2:9); 14:1, the Lamb "standing on Mount Zion" (see Ps. 2:6).[23] Whether or not these parallels qualify as a sustained exposition of that Psalm, it is certainly true that the latter half of the Revelation can be characterized as John's answer to the question of the psalmist, "Why do the nations rage, and the people imagine vain things?" (Ps. 2:1).

It is also evident that John uses Daniel 7:3–7 in his description of the Beast coming out of the sea in chapter 13. It is as if Daniel's terrible fourth beast (Dan. 7:7) is now seen encompassing in itself the other three (13:2). Like Daniel's fourth beast, it has ten horns (Dan. 7:7, 24), but unlike anything in Daniel's visions it also has seven heads.[24] The Beast of Revelation 13 can hardly be understood apart from the Dragon of chapter 12, a figure with no real counterpart in

---

22. For a similar conclusion, see Frederick D. Mazzaferri, *The Genre of the Book of Revelation from a Source-Critical Perspective*, BZNW 54 (Berlin: Walter de Gruyter, 1989), 271–74, 295–96.

23. Caird, *Commentary*, 141–42, 149–50, 178; see also 12:10, "the kingdom of our God and the authority of his Christ" (compare Ps. 2:2).

24. It has been suggested that since the third of Daniel's beasts had four heads (Dan 7:6), and the others (so far as we know!) had one apiece, the seven heads are simply the total of the four. This obviously is a farfetched interpretation!

the Book of Daniel. The Dragon too has "seven heads and ten horns" (12:3). When John encounters these details again in his vision of the Beast, they are already familiar to him and his readers. The Dragon of 12:3–4 and the woman of verses 1–2 must be interpreted together, for they are introduced in parallel fashion as great "signs" that "appeared in heaven" (12:1, 3). The conflict between these two figures precedes all the other conflicts described in Revelation 13–20.

Because of the way in which the conflict is described, some scholars have come to see it as a transformation, not of an ancient text, but of a myth. There was in virtually every culture of the Mediterranean world some variation of a common mythic pattern involving combat between a hero and a monster. In most cases there is also a goddess who is either the hero's wife or mother, and who accompanies the hero as his ally or the monster's potential victim. One of the closest parallels is the Greek myth of Leto, a woman pregnant by Zeus who is pursued by Python, who intends to kill her. She is protected by the north wind and by Poseidon, god of the sea. She gives birth to Apollo and Artemis, and Apollos grows up to defeat Python and finally to establish the Pythian games. In Egypt there is Isis, pregnant by Osiris, who gives birth to Horus. She and her child are pursued by Seth-Typhon, who tries to kill the child. But Isis is aided by Ra and Thoth, and finally Horus defeats the evil Seth-Typhon and becomes King.[25] One way of reading Revelation 12 is simply as an early Christian variant of one of these widely known myths.

Evidence within the chapter, however, points toward a different—though not incompatible—understanding of John's vision. The Dragon is identified by the reliable narrator in 12:9 as "the ancient serpent, who is called the devil, and Satan, who deceives the whole earth." The term, "the ancient serpent" recalls the narrative of Eve and the serpent in Genesis 3, even though the explicit identification of the serpent as the devil, and Satan was not made by the writer of Genesis.

---

25. For a full discussion of these and other forms of the combat myth, and convenient reference to relevant primary sources, see Adela Yarbro Collins, *The Combat Myth in the Book of Revelation*, Harvard Dissertations in Religion 9 (Missoula, Mont.: Scholars, 1976), 57–100.

John's reference to the "seed" (σπέρμα) of the woman (12:17) is odd because *seed* was normally used (as the English cognate *sperm*, suggests) of a father's offspring rather than a mother's. Yet Genesis 3 refers to a woman's "seed" when, in his judgment on the serpent, God says, "And I will put enmity between you and the woman, and between your seed and her seed; he will strike your head, and you will strike his heel." In the only other New Testament interpretation of this text, the serpent is understood to be Satan, while the seed of the woman are understood as Christian believers: "The God of peace," Paul writes, "will soon crush Satan under your feet" (Rom. 16:20; see also Luke 10:19). In Revelation 12 the serpent is also Satan (v. 9), while the seed of the woman is understood first as the Child (Jesus) appointed to "shepherd all the nations with a rod of iron" (v. 5); the "rest of her seed" are Christian believers, as in Romans, those who "keep the commands of God and have the testimony of Jesus" (v. 17).

If Genesis 3:15 is the proper point of reference, then there is an actual text behind chapters 12–13, not just an unwritten cycle of traditions. These two chapters are not so much a myth as a *midrash*. In Judaism a midrash was an expanded paraphrase of an authoritative text, usually from the Hebrew Bible. In this instance, John's vision expands a single text (Gen. 3:15) into an extraordinary two-stage account of an apocalyptic struggle between good and evil. Chapter 12 details the enmity between the serpent (the Dragon) and the woman; chapter 13, the enmity between the serpent's "seed" (the Beast from the sea) and the "seed" of the woman (Christian believers). It is no accident, therefore, that one of the Beast's heads is "as slain [ὡς ἐσφαγμένην, *hōs esphagmenēn*] to death, and his mortal wound was healed" (13:3; see also vv. 12, 14). Words spoken long ago to the serpent in Genesis, "he will strike your head," come true in John's vision.

To be sure, not everything works out consistently. The student still will be left with questions. Why, for example, is the head of the Beast wounded instead of the Dragon's or serpent's head, as Genesis 3:15 would lead us to expect? Moreover, something is missing between stage one and stage two of the conflict. In chapter 12 the conflict is primarily between the Dragon and the woman, as the midrash requires (12:4b–6, 13–17). Even though the child is at first the object of the Dragon's evil intent, he is protected by being taken to heaven and is effectively removed from the story. In chapter 13 the Beast continues the Dragon's warfare not against the child, but against the rest of the woman's seed (see the expression, "to make war," in 12:17 and 13:7).

Such questions are not explicitly answered, but it is important to remember that in chapter 5 the Lamb, like the Beast from the sea, was introduced "as slain" (ὡς ἐσφαγμένην, 5:6; also 13:3). Both the Lamb and the Beast have the "battle scars" of a confrontation never recounted.[26] This confrontation can only be the death of Jesus on the cross. The logic of John's use of Genesis 3:15 suggests that this event was also the wounding of the Beast.[27] Yet it is a presupposition of chapters 12–13, rather than part of the actual story line. The Lamb appears in these chapters only in a song of praise about those who conquered the Dragon "by the blood of the Lamb and by the word of their testimony" (12:11). The unspoken assumption is that the Lamb and the woman's child are the same.

Two questions remain. First, who is the woman who bore the child? Second, who is the Beast from the sea? These questions are not so easily answered as commentators imply. In the ancient text John is rewriting, the woman has not yet been named (only in Gen. 3:20 is she given the name "Eve . . . the mother of all the living"). She is simply "the woman," and in Revelation her male child is a human being, "born of woman" (compare the use of that phrase in Job 14:1; Matt. 11:11; Gal. 4:4). With her child, she faces the power of evil. The child is snatched up to God, while she is kept safe in the desert, protected even by the earth, in a place that God has prepared for her (12:6, 13–17). This is John's version of the familiar myth, shaped decisively by his midrash on Genesis 3:15. Clearly, the Revelation is not interested in identifying this woman more precisely, and there is something to be said for leaving it at that (see discussion of *sexuality*, pp. 137–139).

---

26. The Book of Revelation makes no attempt to interpret the words, "you will strike his heel," in Gen. 3:15 (as, for example, in Rom. 16:20 and Luke 10:19). It is doubtful, for example, that this text is in view in the reference to "trampling the winepress of God's wrath" in 19:15.

27. This conclusion has some features in common with that of Paul S. Minear, *I Saw a New Earth* (Washington, D.C.: Corpus, 1968), 247–60, though Minear, strangely enough, made his case without reference to Gen. 3:15.

One common line of interpretation sees the woman of chapter 12, like the prostitute of chapter 17 and the bride of chapter 21, as a metaphor for a city, or community of people. Some would link the twelve stars in the woman's crown to the twelve tribes of Israel or the twelve apostles of Christ (see Joseph's dream of the sun, moon, and twelve stars in Gen. 37:9). More important, the comparison of the people of God to a woman in labor is found in a number of biblical and early Jewish texts, such as Isaiah 9:6–7; 26:17–18, and 66:7–9, and Micah 4:10, and the hymns from Qumran.[28] Such parallels could suggest that the woman is "Zion" (Isa. 66:8; see also the early Christian text, 4 Ezra 2:40), possibly an idealization of Israel or Jerusalem. It is clear in any case that the woman of chapter 12 cannot be identified quite so confidently as can the Dragon (in v. 9), or the male Child who will "rule the nations with a rod of iron" (v. 5), for no reliable narrator has told us who she is. The student, left to choose between a general and a more specific interpretation, may find there is wisdom in leaving the door open to both options.

The same is true of the Beast in chapter 13. Most commentators assume that the Beast is identified in the text in two ways: first, by the enigmatic "number of a man," 666, assigned to it in 13:18, and, second, by the detailed interpretation supplied in 17:7–18 (see pp. 102–103). The result is a highly political identification, as either the Roman Empire of John's day or one specific emperor to come, understood as "Nero brought back to life" (Nero Redivivus, see pp. 45–46). This interpretation assumes that the mystery, or explanation, given by a reliable narrator in 17:7–18 is the key to understanding both the vision John has just seen in 17:1–6 and the vision of chapter 13. Yet the angel explicitly limits the explanation to the former ("the woman and the Beast that carries her and has the seven heads and the ten horns," 17:7). Few would say that this is the woman in chapter 12 (see p. 100), but the Beast is recognizable as the Beast of chapter 13 by the reference to his heads and horns and his "names of blasphemy" (see 13:1). The description is carried no further. Nothing corresponds to 13:2–5; instead the Beast's color is specified as "scarlet" (17:3), anticipating the "purple and scarlet" of the woman (17:4; compare 18:16).

---

28. 1QH 3.3–18; see Collins, *Combat Myth*, 67–68.

No one will want to argue that this is an altogether different Beast from the one who rose out of the sea in chapter 13. But do not read chapter 13 with the interpretations given in chapter 17 already in mind. This is cheating. The student should try to read the text of Revelation in the same way in which John saw his visions—as if for the first time. Just as the figure who appeared to John in chapter 1 should not be understood as Jesus until he so identifies himself in the text, so the Beast in chapter 13 should not be assumed prematurely to represent the Roman Empire. When chapter 13 is interpreted "from within" (in the context of John's midrash on Gen. 3:15) instead of "from without" (from the perspective of chapter 17), the Beast takes on a slightly different, less political, shape.

Nero did not suffer his mortal wound as a result of Jesus Christ's death on the cross, and in fact the "wounded head" of the Beast is not even mentioned in chapter 17. The contexts of chapters 12–13, and of the midrash on Genesis favors a somewhat more generalized interpretation of the Beast, just as it favors a rather generalized interpretation of the pregnant woman. Perhaps the most that can be said on the basis of chapters 12–13 alone is that the Beast is the agent, or historical expression on earth, of the Dragon (Satan), in much the same way that the Lamb is the agent, or historical expression on earth, of "the One sitting on the throne." Significantly, it is "to God and to his throne" that the child in chapter 12 is taken for protection. The interpretation supplied in chapter 17 establishes the Beast's identity *in relation to the political and social world of John's day*. Certainly this process begins in chapter 13 in the figure of the second Beast, "from the earth" (13:11–18, "the false prophet" of 16:13; 19:20; 20:10), and above all in the much-discussed number *666* (13:18),[29] but only in chapter 17 is it carried through consistently.

---

29. There will probably never be agreement among scholars on the solution to this riddle. It is possible to give *666* either a concrete interpretation (for example, as the total of the numerical value of the letters in the title "Nero Caesar"—but only when written in Hebrew!) or a more general one (for example, as falling three times short of *7*, the number representing perfection). Although its significance should not be exaggerated, enterprising students may want to tackle it (See, for example, Henry B. Swete, *The Apocalypse of St. John* (London: Macmillan, 1922), 172–73; Robert H. Mounce, *The Book of Revelation*, New International Commentary on the New Testament (Grand Rapids: Eerdmans, 1977), 263–65; Caird, *Commentary*, 174–77; Minear, *I Saw*, 256–60.

The hermeneutical question this leaves us with is whether the concrete identification remains as binding on the twentieth-century interpreter as on John. Must the Beast be understood *only* as the Roman Empire, either in the past or in some revived form, or can the earthly expression of Satan's power find a different identity, whether institutional or personal, in a different time? The recognition of a certain distinction between the portrayals of the Beast in chapters 13 and 17 may open the door for some students to a more general application of John's vision to their own time. Compare the general application of the Antichrist in 1 John 2:18 and 2 John 7. We will consider more such hermeneutical questions in chapter 8.

## The Millstone

So far we have given all our attention to John's transformation of the Hebrew Bible, which was his sacred text and the reference point for virtually everything he saw and wrote. Occasionally, however, the words of Jesus serve as his point of departure. For example, a refrain in the seven messages of chapters 2–3 is a formula known to us from the Gospels: "Whoever has ears let him hear." In the Revelation what must be heard is "what the Spirit says to the churches" (2:6, 11, 17, 29; 3:6, 13, 22; compare 13:9). It is no accident that it is Jesus, the narrator in these chapters, who uses the phrase. Other examples include 3:3 ("If you do not stay awake, I will come as a thief, and you will not know in what hour I will come upon you"), 16:15 ("Behold, I come as a thief. Blessed is the one who stays awake and keeps his garments;" see Mark 13:25–37; Matt. 24:42, 25:13; Luke 12:37–40), and 3:5 ("I will confess his name before my Father and before his angels," see Matt. 10:32; Luke 12:8). While the use of the Gospel tradition in the Book of Revelation is a worthwhile subject for study, the use of these traditions is fairly direct, with little transformation or reinterpretation. The risen Jesus simply repeats what the earthly Jesus was remembered to have said.

Revelation 18:21 is an interesting exception, both because Jesus is not the one speaking and because the allusion to Jesus' words is combined with an allusion to a biblical text. Here we meet again "a strong angel" (εἷς ἄγγελος ἰσχυρός, *heis angelos ischyros*), recalling once more the strong angel of 5:2 and of 10:1. This time the angel lifts high "a stone, like a great millstone" and throws it into the sea, saying, "Thus violently the great city of Babylon will be thrown, and will be found no more" (18:21). One text probably in view is Jeremiah 51:63–64, where Jeremiah had written a scroll about judgment on Babylon (the literal Babylon of his day) and was told to read it aloud in Babylon, tie a stone to it, and throw it in the Euphrates, saying "So will Babylon sink to rise no more!"

There is, however, a text in the Gospels where Jesus said, "Whoever offends one of these little ones who believe in me, it would be better for him to have a millstone [μύλος ὀνικός] put around his neck and be thrown into the sea" (Mark 9:42; also Matt. 18:6; Luke 17:2). The text from Jeremiah is obviously part of the background to the text in Revelation because of its direct reference to "Babylon," yet it is also significant that the strong angel's pronouncement of doom in Revelation 18 leads up to the statement that in Babylon "the blood of prophets and saints was found, and of all who were slain on the earth" (18:24). Babylon the Great is thrown into the sea for one main reason: because she harmed the "little ones" who belonged to Jesus! The saying of Jesus is here transformed into a vision and acted out in a violent and unforgettable drama.

These examples illustrate only a few of the ways in which John's visions transformed earlier texts and traditions. The student will encounter this phenomenon in virtually every text in Revelation, especially in chapters 4–22. The terminology does not matter. We can call it intertextuality, the current buzz word, or tradition history, reminding us of the rather different procedures by which we study the Gospels, or we can call it midrash, or exegesis (raising the question of how similar our exegesis of John should be to John's exegesis of his biblical texts). Whatever term we use, we must take careful account of this phenomenon in interpreting the Book of Revelation.

# 8

# Theological Interpretation: The Horizons of Patmos

Most of our discussion has centered around John's visions and the manner in which he described them. Only briefly did we raise the question of what John's visions were about (see pp. 49–50). There we found it difficult to see references in Revelation to specific persons or events in the political history of John's day, much less use these to determine precisely when "John's day" was (A.D. 70–100 is a rather wide range!). The question not yet addressed is what the Book of Revelation is about *theologically*. This question is significant, though many interpreters make the mistake of raising it prematurely. I have deferred the question to our last chapter, but not with the purpose of avoiding it. We must address the question, or we will be like the student who knew what the learned mathematician was saying but not what she was saying it about!

When we ask what the Revelation is about theologically, we no longer simply listen to the text in its own terms but now bring to it *our* questions. We take the liberty to ask John and the voices he heard from heaven to respond to *our* agenda. There is nothing wrong with this so long as we acknowledge what we are doing and do not force answers from the text where there are none. Theological interpretation in this case is a kind of dialogue with the text that attempts to find out the horizons of Patmos. How far could John see from his lonely island, and what did he see?

At the very least, traditional Christian theology asks two questions of any work: "What does it tell us about Jesus Christ?" and "What does it tell us about ourselves?" Given the nature of this book, the question about ourselves leads naturally and inevitably to a third question: "What does this work tell us about our future and, indeed, about the future of the world?" The first question concerns what theologians call *christology*; the second is about *ecclesiology* (the study of the *ecclesia* or church); the third concerns *eschatology*.

## Christology

Revelation undeniably has a christology. It begins by describing itself as "a revelation of Jesus Christ" (1:1). Grammatically, "Jesus Christ" could be understood either as the content of the revelation, making it a revelation *about* Jesus, or as its source, making it a revelation *from* Jesus. The fact that the book's content is designated in 1:1 as "the things that must happen soon" suggests that Jesus is understood here as the source.

Revelation is primarily about the future, not about Jesus, yet in the course of its visions several distinct and memorable portraits of Jesus emerge. Even before the visions, John sends his readers grace and peace "from Jesus Christ, the faithful witness, the firstborn of the dead, and ruler of the kings of the earth" (1:5). This formula, which may have been developed among early Christians even before John wrote, looks like a *transformation* (in the sense described in pp. 107–109) of several phrases from Psalm 89. "Firstborn" from Psalm 89:27 has become "firstborn of the dead" in light of Jesus' resurrection (see Col. 1:18). "Highest among the kings of the earth" from the same verse has become "ruler of the kings of the earth" in light of Jesus' role in the latter half of the book. "Faithful witness" from Psalm 89:37 has been transformed from a reference to the moon as a witness in the skies to God's eternal covenant with David into a reference to the faithfulness of Jesus to the message for which he died (see 3:14). Psalm 89 is a psalm about the line of descent from King David, and it appears that John's starting point is the notion that Jesus is the Jewish Messiah, or anointed king, from that eternal line.

This is even more evident in 5:5, where one of the elders in heaven tells John that the one who has "conquered" and is therefore worthy to open the seven-sealed scroll is "the Lion who is of the tribe of Judah, the root of David." But the Lion, when he appears on the scene, has been transformed into a "Lamb standing as one slain, having seven heads and seven eyes, which are the seven spirits of God sent into all the earth" (5:6). We noted in chapter 6 (p. 99) how the *reliable narrator* identified the seven eyes of the Lamb as the seven spirits of God. More striking, however, is something that did not come into our earlier discussion: A reliable narrator has also told us in advance the identity of the one opening the seals. He would be *the Lion of Judah* and *a descendant of David* (the Davidic Messiah). The explanation *preceded* the vision. Yet we will always remember Jesus in the Book of Revelation as *the slain Lamb*, not as the Lion of Judah. It is consistently the Lamb who opens the seals and who carries out the judgments of "the One sitting on the throne."

For once the reliable narrator has not had the last word! The explanation was given in advance to interpret the vision, yet John's vision of the Lamb interprets in turn and qualifies the explanation. This means that the figures of the Lion and the Lamb interpret each other. If the Lion turns out to be a sacrificial Lamb, the Lamb through the rest of the book behaves very much like a Lion (for example, in 6:17; 17:14). Jesus will do what the Davidic Messiah (on the basis of Psalm 2) was expected to do. He will "strike the nations and shepherd them with a rod of iron" (19:15; see also 2:26–28; 12:5). But the Revelation contributes to the tradition something new, the distinctly Christian notion that the Messiah accomplishes what he came to do only as a result of being slain.

For the most part, Jesus Christ is incognito between John's introductory material (1:2, 5, 9) and his concluding words to the churches after the visions are over (22:16–21). Only in certain set phrases such as "the testimony of Jesus" (12:17; 19:10; 20:4; see also 17:6), or the "faith of Jesus" (14:12) is he mentioned by name within the visions proper.[1] Elsewhere he appears as the slain Lamb (twenty-nine references in all), as the male child born of the woman (12:5), and at least twice as an angelic figure (1:12–16; 19:11–16). His identity as Jesus is no secret in any of these passages,[2] yet in his last decisive appearance (19:11–16) John calls him

---

1. The title *Christ* occurs four times within the visions (11:15; 12:10; 20:4, 6), always with the definite article and probably as a title, "the Messiah," rather than as a name. In 11:15 and 12:10 the title appears to come directly from Ps. 2:2.

by a variety of names ("Faithful and True," v. 11; "the Word of God," v. 13; "King of kings and Lord of lords," v. 16) and suggests in verse 12 that his real name is known only to himself.[3]

Besides being a christology of the Lion and of the Lamb, John's is, to a degree unrecognized by most students of the book, an *angel christology*. Jesus appears twice in the form of an angel (chaps. 1 and 19) and appoints an angel to be his representative (22:16: "I, Jesus, sent my angel to testify these things to you for the churches"; see 1:1 and 22:6, where God does the sending). This is the angel who has just shown John the vision of the new Jerusalem (21:9–22:9), and possibly the same one who showed and explained to him the vision of Babylon the prostitute (17:1–19:10). Unlike the angel of chapter 1, these angels refused to accept John's worship (19:10; 22:9; contrast 1:17). Each is simply part of the sequence of seven angels who had poured out the seven bowls of God's wrath on the earth. Yet they served their purpose as reliable narrators through John's last two visions and gave place at the end to the one narrative voice behind the many interpretive voices throughout the book—the voice of Jesus himself.

While these angels are clearly distinguished from Jesus, they can be regarded as his surrogates or agents, extensions of his presence into John's visions. The same is true of the "strong angel" of 10:1–2, the figure "like a son of man" seated on a cloud in 14:14, and the angel who "tramples the great winepress of God's anger" in 14:19–20. *Functionally* they are all equivalent to Jesus. What they do is what Jesus himself does. Compare the association common in the Gospel tradition between "the Son of Man" and "his angels," for example, in Mark 13:26–27 and Matthew 24:30–31; Mark 8:38 and Matthew 13:41; 16:27, and 25:31.

---

2. He identifies himself as the *risen One* in 1:18, while the designation *King of kings* and *Lord of lords* in 19:16 links him unmistakably to the Lamb (see 17:14). Moreover, the "sharp, two- edged sword coming out of his mouth" (1:16; 19:15) is strong evidence that the mounted figure in chap. 19 is indeed the same as the figure on foot in chap. 1. Similarly, the notion that he will "strike the nations" with his sword and "shepherd them with a rod of iron" (19:15) corresponds to the destiny of the child born of the woman in 12:5.

3. See the "new name" of Jesus (3:12), and the "new name" given the victorious believer, "which no one knows except the one receiving" (2:17).

Above all, angels in the Book of Revelation speak. With John and his fellow prophets, they have the "testimony of Jesus" (19:10). As we have seen (p. 52), Jesus in the form of an angel speaks continuously from 1:17b through 3:20. By contrast, Jesus as the Lamb never speaks a word in the entire book. We are reminded of the suffering servant in Isaiah who, like a lamb, "did not open his mouth" (Isa. 53:7; see 1 Pet. 2:22–23). The Lamb is silent—as silent in triumph as in death. His role is not to speak but to act, and his supreme act is the shedding of his blood (1:5b; 5:9; 7:14; 12:11; 19:13). This is the uniqueness of Jesus the Lamb in Revelation, for this unites him not with angels but with human beings; they too are victorious precisely in their deaths.

If we look at the Book of Revelation for its account of the triumph of Jesus Christ over the powers of evil, then its angel christology is significant, for angels are consistently the instruments of divine judgment. Angels, along with Jewish expectations of a Messiah from the line of David, shape even the way in which the Lamb is portrayed. But if Christians are looking for a christology to serve as the basis for their own self-understanding, the figure of the slain Lamb is decisive. Ironically, the slaughter of the Lamb is a presupposition of the book, not part of its actual story line. This is a prophetic letter, after all, and not a Gospel. Yet the cross of Jesus is as decisive here as it is in the Gospels or the letters of Paul, for the shedding of blood defines both the Lamb's identity and that of his followers.

## Martyrdom

After "christology" we come to "ecclesiology," yet there is no particular awareness in Revelation of the *church* in the universal sense of Ephesians or Colossians. John writes only to specific Asian churches as congregations (1:4, 11, 20; 22:16) and to individuals within these congregations. Therefore, the question of ecclesiology has to be posed more simply: "What does this book tell us about ourselves?" Here is where the theologians' terms must yield to those derived from the book itself.

The personal application, of course, depends on where we stand in the great conflict between good and evil. Are we with the Lamb or the Beast? The conflict is described in such a way as to make neutrality difficult. As readers we are drawn into the action in spite of ourselves. If we have read the book before—perhaps even if we have not—we know who is going to win, yet even the most stubborn among us will not be indifferent about the outcome. There is nothing subtle or ambivalent about the conflict. Evil may masquerade as good. The Beast may be slain and then healed like the Lamb (13:3). Another Beast may have horns like the Lamb, but his speech betrays him. The Lamb does not speak, but this figure does—with the voice of the Dragon (13:11). Others may be deceived (13:14), but the reader is not. The distinction between good and evil is sharply drawn, and good triumphs in the end. It is the kind of story we enjoyed as children, and the kind many of us, whether we admit it or not, still prefer as adults.

Yet, something is wrong. Jesus Christ triumphs in the Book of Revelation, but at what cost? The people of God are introduced for the first time in John's visions of the future as "the souls of those *slain* for the Word of God and for the testimony they had" (6:9). These "souls" are "under the altar" (presumably in heaven) crying out to God to "judge" and "avenge our *blood* from the dwellers on the earth." They are given white robes and told to "rest a little while until [the number of] their fellow servants and brothers who are to be *killed* as they were is complete" (vv. 9–11). The italicized words point explicitly to violent death. Like the Lamb, these individuals have been slain, and as the Lion of Judah "conquered" (5:5), they too await their time of victory and vindication. In other words, they are martyrs.

These martyrs, or a group like them, are seen again in chapter 7. A number is announced, 144,000, of those "sealed, from every tribe of Israel's sons," but what John sees instead is an innumerable multitude from every nation standing before the throne and the Lamb. The 144,000 Jews have been transformed, just as the Lion of Judah was transformed into the Lamb.[4] The multitude is "dressed in white robes and with palm branches in their hands" (7:9) and identified as "those who have come out of the great persecution, and have washed their robes and made them white in the blood of the Lamb"

---

4. See Robert H. Gundry, "The New Jerusalem: People as Place, not Place for People," *Novum Testamentum* 29 (1987): 260.

(7:14). Although it is not said how they "came out of the great perse-cution," martyrdom seems the implication. In a later vision, the mul-titude appears as 144,000 "virgins" (14:4), with the Lamb's name on their foreheads (compare 22:4). They have been "redeemed from the earth" and have "followed the Lamb wherever he went" (14:1–5). The number suggests completeness (144,000 = 12 x 12 x 1000), raising the question of whether this can be the full number of martyrs to which 6:11 refers. There always will be different views of the identity of these groups and their relationship to each other, yet it is clear that all in some way depict for John the people of God.[5]

The hint of violent death followed by vindication becomes explicit in other passages. This is the case in the account of the two "witnesses" (lit. "martyrs") in chapter 11. When the period of their testimony is over, "the Beast who comes out of the abyss will *make war* with them and *conquer* them and *kill* them, and their bodies [will lie] on the street of the great city, which is called spiritually 'Sodom' and 'Egypt,' where also their Lord was crucified" (11:7–8). They are raised from the dead and vindicated against their enemies (vv. 11–12). Similarly in chapter 13 the Beast is given authority "to *make war* with the saints and *conquer* them" (13:7), so that John writes of them, "If anyone is for captivity, to captivity he goes; if anyone is to be *killed* by the sword, by the sword he is *killed*" (13:10). By chapter 15 the tables are turned. John sees beside the sea of glass in heaven "those who conquer from [by escaping] the Beast, and from his image, and from the number of his name" (15:2).

In the context of Revelation, this does not mean that they were somehow refugees or survivors. The implication is rather that, like the Lamb, they conquered the Beast through death itself. A song in 16:6 refers to those who "shed the *blood* of saints and prophets," while the prostitute in chapter 17 is described as "drunk from the *blood* of the saints and from the *blood* of the witnesses [martyrs] of Jesus" (17:6). In Babylon "the *blood* of prophets and saints was found, and of all who were *slain* on the earth" (18:24). Such texts stand as evidence that the "conquerors" or "those who overcome,"

---

5. Some, for example, identify the 144,000, either in chap. 7 or in chaps. 7 and 14, as Jews or Jewish Christians, and the innumerable multitude as Gentile Christians, but it is doubtful that the distinction was as significant to John as it is to modern interpreters.

to whom specific blessings are promised in each of the seven messages of chapters 2–3, are actually those who, like the Lamb, conquer through death (3:21; 5:5–6).

Most significant, those who "lived and reigned with the Christ for a thousand years" are described not simply as "the church," or as those who "believed in Jesus," but as "the souls of those *beheaded* for the testimony of Jesus and for the word of God, and such as did not worship the Beast or his image and did not receive his mark on their forehead and on their hand" (20:4). They are recognizably the same group as the "souls under the altar" first introduced in 6:9–11 in connection with the fifth seal. There they had cried out for God to judge in their favor (κρίνεις, 6:10), and now John sees a "judgment given for them" (κρίμα ἐδόθη αὐτοῖς, krima edothē autois, 20:4a). Their prayer has been answered. Theirs is the "first resurrection" (20:5). They are given new life, and the privilege of reigning with the Christ (see also 5:10; 22:5).

The often asked question of whether those who reign for a thousand years are the whole church or only the martyrs rests on a false distinction. In the Revelation, the whole church is a *martyr church* both in the broad sense of bearing testimony to Jesus (the Greek word μαρτυρία, *martyria*, means *witness*), and in the narrower sense of being put to death for that testimony.

There is no plausible way to distinguish between those "beheaded for the testimony of Jesus" and those who "did not worship the Beast or his image" (20:4), as if the latter group had somehow managed to escape death at the Beast's hands. The only distinction John seems to know is between the "witnesses [martyrs] of Jesus" and the "saints." The difference is not that the witnesses are killed and the saints are spared. Within John's horizons at least, both groups suffer death. John probably understands the witnesses as prophets or special custodians of the Christian message and the saints as all other faithful Christians.[6] John, after all, was a "charis-

6. John's understanding of witnesses as prophets can be seen from a comparison of 16:6 ("saints and prophets") with 17:6 ("saints" and "witnesses of Jesus"), or from a comparison of 22:9 ("your brothers the prophets") with 19:10a ("your brothers who have the testimony of Jesus"), on the ground that "the testimony of Jesus is the spirit of prophecy" (19:10b). The saints might then be understood as "those who keep the words of this book" (22:9; compare 1:3). Even this distinction, however, should not be pressed too rigidly.

matic," in the sense that authority in the churches rested with the prophets—including himself.

Within John's horizons, *martyr* is not a technical term for those unfortunate individuals who happen to be killed. Rather, it defines the very nature and existence of the church. The recognition of this should put to rest the claims of some scholars that the Revelation is a *triumphalist* book. Victory is indeed a major theme, but victory comes in the same way it comes in the experience of Paul (2 Cor. 4:10–11), or in Peter (1 Pet. 4:13), or in the teaching of Jesus (Mark 8:34–35; Matt. 23:12, and Luke 14:11). Victory comes through suffering and death. What counts in the end is not simply believing in Jesus, but in "following the Lamb wherever he went" (14:4)—the path of discipleship, suffering, and death. No one can teach, preach, or even seriously study the Revelation without recognizing how deeply it contradicts all our dominant cultural values of wealth, success, and power.

## Sexuality

The student has yet another surprise in store in connection with the identity of those who belong to Jesus. They are male! The same passage (14:1–5) in which the 144,000 are described as "redeemed from the earth," "blameless," and as those who "followed the Lamb wherever he went," also calls them "virgins" (v. 4).[7] The term "virgin," more commonly applied in our culture to women, is here defined as "those who have not defiled themselves with women"—clearly implying that they are male virgins.

Most of the visions in the book are seen from a male perspective. John was a man, living in a male-dominated culture. He perceived the figures in his visions as different from himself, as animals (a lamb, a dragon, a serpent, two beasts, and four living creatures), or as angelic or divine figures,[8] or as women. John saw the three women in his visions in the same three roles in which men in virtu-

---

7. See Adela Yarbro Collins, *Crisis and Catharsis: The Power of the Apocalypse* (Louisville: Westminster-John Knox, 1984), 127–31.

8. Even though an angel twice assures him by claiming to be only his "fellow servant," John's own initial perception of the angel was as a divine being worthy of worship (19:10; 22:8–9).

ally every culture perceive the women in their lives—as mother (chap. 12), as prostitute or temptress (chap. 17), and as bride, or wife (chap. 21). The reference to the 144,000 virgins in chapter 14 is to be understood as a warning in advance, applicable to both men and women, against Babylon the prostitute, not as a renunciation of marriage. The use of marriage and the wedding feast in chapters 19 and 21 as a metaphor for salvation makes it unlikely that the expression, "to defile oneself with women," can refer to the marriage relationship.

The feminist reading of Revelation has led some readers to put the book aside as a limited and distorted version of Christianity, or worse, as a typical example of Christian male chauvinism. But feminists, Christian or otherwise, should not give up too quickly. The women in John's visions, unlike the animals and the angels, represent communities of people, good and bad, rather than God or supernatural powers or even human institutions. The mother of chapter 12 is either the human community to which all belong or the community of women who preserve and nurture it or, more specifically, the Jewish community from which the Messiah came. The prostitute of chapter 17 is the city of Rome, or more broadly, the community of those who give Rome their allegiance. The bride of chapter 21 is Jerusalem, "the holy city . . . coming down out of heaven from God" (vv. 1, 9), a city understood, not as a place, but as a people.[9]

John's three women create a transformation as marked as that of the Lion or the 144,000. The reader was first invited to identify *himself* as one born of woman, like the male child destined to "shepherd the nations with a rod of iron" (12:5, 17; also 2:26–27). Next, the identification is with young men resisting the temptations of the prostitute (14:4; compare 18:4). In the third instance, however, *he* cannot take on, even in imagination, the role of bridegroom. That role belongs to the Lamb, and to him alone (19:7, 9; 21:9). Unlike the suffering of death and the execution of judgment and rule over the nations, the bridegroom's role is not one that Christ can share with his people, for this is his role *toward* his people. There is a mutuality in these images found nowhere else in the Revelation. This mutuality "feminizes" the church and the believer. The bride's "fine linen,"

---

9. See Gundry, "The New Jerusalem," 254–64.

the reliable narrator has told us, is "the righteousness of the saints" (19:8), and we can only conclude from that identification that the bride herself is none other than the victorious saints. *Her* true identity is not that of a priest or warrior or male virgin but of a bride and wife (the imagery of Eph. 5:25–27). The reader, regardless of sex, is placed abruptly in the role of the woman! The author of 1 John writes, "It does not yet appear what we shall be, but we know that when it does appear we will be like him, for we will see him as he is" (3:2). There is no need either to assume or rule out common authorship of 1 John and Revelation, but what "appears" in Revelation is that the church is "like" Jesus in much the same sense that Eve was "like" Adam (Gen. 2:20–24). *She* is his counterpart and his partner in ruling the new earth.

It is difficult to determine whether women were included among the prophets who were John's "fellow servants" in the congregations from which he came and to which he wrote (for example, whether "brothers" in 19:10 and 22:9 is generic or specifically male). Ironically, the only false prophet denounced individually anywhere in the book is a woman ("Jezebel, who calls herself a prophetess," 2:20). What seems to have made her prophecies false, however, was their content ("immorality and eating food sacrificed to idols"), not the fact that she was a woman. The congregations addressed in Revelation were prophetic and millenarian, and in such congregations throughout Christian history the ministry of women has often played a prominent role. These are issues to which the book does not speak because it is more interested in the church's symbolic identity and faithfulness in the face of evil than in her daily life and liturgy.

## Eschatology

Appropriately, we come last to eschatology. Most students will agree that eschatology, in the sense of "what must happen soon" (1:1; 22:6) or "what will happen afterward" (1:19) is what the book is finally about—certainly more than sexuality, more than martyrdom, more than the church, and more even than Jesus Christ. But when is, or was, "soon"? When is "afterward"? Are the things to come still to come, or are they here? Or has the time for them come and gone? The greatest hermeneutical problem facing the student is the stubborn fact that we are reading the book 1900 years after it was written. I have left these questions to the last, not because they are unimportant, but because students are least likely to reach a consensus here. These questions cannot be fully answered from within the Revelation itself. Answers tend to come from without, from the interpreter's presuppositions brought to the reading of the text. For this reason, I offer only a few very general guidelines to suggest ways in which the text itself can sometimes resist predetermined interpretations.

### The Rapture and the Tribulation

One school of thought called *dispensationalism* has traditionally assumed that Revelation 4–22 depicts a series of actual future events in the precise order of John's visions. Most dispensationalists assume, on the basis of Paul's teaching in 1 Thess. 4:17 about a "rapture" (a taking up to heaven) of all Christians, that the church is already in heaven when the sequence of visions begins in 4:1. Consequently, those throughout the book who "have the word of God and the testimony of Jesus" and are martyred for their faith are *not* the Christians to whom John was writing, but a Jewish remnant (with possibly some non-Jews as well) converted to faith in Jesus *after* the church is taken from the scene!

The effect of this "pretribulation rapture" is to dissociate Christian readers from any persecution and suffering at the hands of the Beast and to deny the church's identity as a martyr church. Yet Paul's "rapture" (from the Latin *rapiemur*, "snatch away," in 1 Thess. 4:17) is simply what the creeds call "the resurrection of the body and the life everlasting" (see v. 16, "the dead in Christ will rise first"), and the Revelation announces this resurrection not in chapter 4 but in chapter 20 ("they came alive and reigned with the Christ for a thousand years," 20:4; "This is the first resurrection," v. 5).

At the same time, there is truth in the notion that the church will be spared the wrath and judgment of God. Jesus promises the church at Philadelphia that "I will keep you from the hour of trial that will come upon the whole world to put to the test the dwellers on the earth" (3:10). The male child in 12:5 is "snatched up to God" from the clutches of the Dragon, and the two witnesses in chapter

11 are taken up to heaven in full view of their enemies just before "the great city" where they were killed is decimated by an earthquake (11:11–13). The so-called "pretribulation rapture" is bound up with the question of what is meant by "the tribulation." Is it the wrath of God poured out on the world in the visions of the trumpets and bowls, or is it the persecution and martyrdom of the faithful at the hands of the Beast and the prostitute? Which is it, for example, in 7:14, the one place in Revelation where the phrase, "the great tribulation," actually occurs? It is wise, so far as possible, to let the book itself define our terms rather than bringing in a set of ready-made definitions from the outside.

Another eschatological issue is the identification of the time period referred to in Revelation 11:2 and 13:5 as "forty-two months," in 11:3 and 12:6 as "1260 days," and in 12:14 as "a time, times, and half a time" (see also Dan. 7:25; 12:7). All three expressions are probably to be understood as equivalent to three and one-half years (half of seven).[10] The implication is that this is a relatively short period of trouble or persecution (12:12, "a little time"), in contrast to the "1000 years" of triumph in chapter 20. Possibly a link is intended between this short time period and the notion expressed in Jesus' eschatological discourse that God has "shortened the days" of tribulation (Mark 13:20) or "great tribulation" (Matt. 24:22) for the sake of his chosen ones. Cutting in half the characteristic number of completeness, 7, achieves the same effect as saying, "It is later than you think," or "The time is near" (1:3; 2:10), or that the last of seven kings "has not yet come, and when he comes he must remain a little while" (17:10). John is saying the end will come *soon* (1:1; 22:6), but not immediately. Dispensationalists have tended to schematize this forty-two months or 1260 days by asking each time it occurs whether it refers to the first half or the latter half of the tribulation period. Yet nothing in any of these texts suggests that the tribulation is seven years in length, or that these time periods were intended to be added together to make seven! Such a notion is derived from the seventy sevens, or weeks of years, in Dan. 9:24–27, on the questionable assumption that John's great tribulation is equivalent to Daniel's seventieth week.

---

10. Prophetic calculations were traditionally based on the assumption of 360 days to a year.

### The Second Coming

Even an event so widely accepted among Christians as the second coming of Jesus Christ is difficult to locate in the Book of Revelation. John affirms its reality almost at the beginning (1:7, "he comes with the clouds, and every eye shall see him"), but does Jesus come "on the clouds" as the angelic figure "like a son of man" in 14:14, or on a "white horse" as the conquering warrior of 19:11–16? Does his coming signal a *rapture* of the saints, or does it precede or follow the rapture? Are there (as the dispensationalists assume) *two* comings, one for the saints and another with the saints, to judge the world? Such questions are more easily answered from our own presuppositions (or imaginations) than from the text of Revelation itself.

### The Millenium and Armageddon

The purpose of these examples is not to disparage the dispensationalists. Most dispensationalists are conscientious interpreters who, because they take the book rather literally, also take it seriously, as John intended. They are no more guilty than others of imposing their own questions and answers on the text. Those in other traditions, for a variety of reasons, often are reluctant to acknowledge what dispensationalists rightly see as central: that Revelation *is* predictive prophecy, a book about the future. Some, wanting to avoid any implication that John was mistaken in claiming that the things he saw were to happen "soon" (1:1; 22:6) or that the time was "near" (1:3; 22:10, 20), have shifted the book's accent from the future realization of Christ's kingdom (11:15) to the church's experience *now* of being "a kingdom, priests to God" (1:6). The notion that "tribulation and kingdom and patience in Jesus" belong to the present (1:9) is used to relieve the problem of the apparent delay in the fulfillment of the specific judgments and blessings John predicted.

A theory as old as Augustine appeals to the principle of reiteration (see pp. 53–55) to argue that the *millennium* mentioned several times in Revelation 20 depicts the triumphant state of the church *now* (spiritually), not a prophecy of the future. It is viewed as either not a millennium at all in the usual sense of the word (*amillennialism*) or a millennium realized in the course of time as a result of the church's mission on earth (*postmillennialism*). In cases where it is acknowledged that those who "reigned with Christ for a thousand years" are, as the text says, those who have died (20:4–5), it is argued that John is not referring to martyrdom and literal resurrection but simply to the natural deaths of Christian believers and their life with Christ in the *intermediate state*.[11] Tempting as it may be to domesticate the book by minimizing its strangeness within the New Testament, it is probably better to acknowledge candidly its unique features (for example, the vision of universal martyrdom and of a future millennial reign) and learn from them. Such recognition can, as we have seen, be a safeguard against the triumphalism sometimes read into parts of this book. Whether for Christ or the Christian, victory comes only through death and resurrection, not through the power of the sword, or even through social action.

This point is missed by those who seize on the term *Armageddon*[12] (Rev. 16:16) as a summons to holy war or an excuse for Christian militancy. There is indeed a battle of Armageddon in Revelation, but it is a unique battle in that its outcome is never for a moment in doubt. The stage is set for it in 16:13–16 and its outcome is clearly stated in advance in 17:14 ("and the Lamb will conquer them, because he is Lord of lords and King of kings, and those who with him are called and chosen and faithful"). Finally, it is recounted in some detail in 19:11–21. It can only be described as "no contest." John makes no effort to maintain even the slightest degree of suspense about who is going to win.

A possible reason is that what John sees depicted here may not be a military conflict at all, but a divine decree or judgment. The victorious figure on the white horse (19:11–16) has his garment already "dipped in blood" (v. 13) because for him the real battle is over (see

---

11. For a vigorous debate on this issue, see Meredith G. Kline, "The First Resurrection" in *Westminster Theological Journal*, hereafter *WTJ*, 37.3 (1975): 366–75, with my own response in *WTJ* 39.1 (1976): 100–09, and Kline's reaffirmation in *WTJ* 39.1 (1976): 110–19.

12. There is no consensus on the meaning of the name *Armageddon*, though it is frequently derived from the Hebrew for "mountain of Megiddo." See Robert H. Mounce, *The Book of Revelation*, New International Commentary on the New Testament (Grand Rapids: Eerdmans, 1977), 301–2. The difficulty that Megiddo, though a famous battlefield, was not a mountain but a plain is lessened if John is speaking paradoxically rather than referring to an actual place.

the "Lamb slain" in 5:6). He wields his sword in a most unusual manner (v. 15; also 1:16), and three of his names are more like names for a decree, or the bearer of a decree, than for a warrior: "Faithful," "True" (v. 11), and "the Word of God" (v. 13). Only "King of kings and Lord of lords" (v. 16; 17:14) fits his military bearing. He recalls more than anything else God's "all-powerful Word" coming down in judgment "from heaven's royal throne" on Egypt in the time of the Exodus—"a fierce warrior in the midst of the doomed land, bearing as a sharp sword your inexorable decree."[13] In Revelation he is unmistakably Jesus, yet in John's vision he is at the same time the embodiment of solemn assurances from the angel that "these are the true words of God" (19:9) or "these words are faithful and true" (21:5; 22:6). He is the "word" of the prophecy coming to realization in visible form as the Word of God, breaking the power of the Beast and providing John and his readers with conclusive assurance that the prophecies are true. The image of Armageddon does *not* imply that Christians are called to take up the sword on Christ's behalf in a holy war, for this has been explicitly forbidden to those who "have ears to hear" (13:9–10).

And what of John's millennium? Some students and scholars are uncomfortable with it because nothing in the Old or New Testament prepares us for it, and because its function seems unclear. Yet as we saw in our discussion of structure (see pp. 67–69), the millennium cannot be made to disappear simply by invoking the principle of reiteration. The battle at the end of the millennium (20:8) cannot be a reenactment of the battle of Armageddon because the Beast and the False Prophet are no longer on the scene. They are still in the lake of fire (v. 10), to which they were consigned a thousand years before! For whatever reason, John's vision makes the point that the Dragon (Satan) is defeated in three stages instead of two. He is thrown first to earth (12:9), then into the abyss (20:1–3), and finally into the lake of fire (20:10).

This can be understood in one of two ways. The first possibility is that the Beast represents only the Roman Empire, and therefore the Beast was destroyed some centuries after the Book of Revelation was written. In this case it has to be candidly admitted that the Beast was not destroyed in anything like the manner John describes in

---

13. *Wisdom of Solomon* 18:15–16.

Revelation 19—although it is of course possible to believe that the Roman Empire came to an end by divine decree! John's vision of the millennium would then be his recognition that the world goes on even after the destruction of the Beast, and that eventually nations will be deceived again (20:3, 8) because Satan was not destroyed but only bound temporarily. Satan has one more card up his sleeve, but when he plays it the outcome will be the same (vv. 7–10). Because all this is at the outer limit of John's horizons, he treats it very briefly and in a somewhat detached way in comparison to his visions of more immediate threats.[14] If labels are important, this is a kind of postmillennial view. Of course it faces the difficulty of knowing what to make of the resurrection of the saints and martyrs at the time the Roman Empire was destroyed!

A second approach assumes that the Beast cannot be identified solely with the Roman Empire of John's day (as chap. 17 might suggest), but that he represents more broadly the historical or institutional expression of evil wherever and whenever it is found (see chap. 13, and its use of Gen. 3:15). Therefore, when the Beast is consigned to the lake of fire (19:20), it means that history as we know it—not just the Roman Empire—has come to an end. Jesus Christ has come to claim his martyred saints and prophets, and rule with them on earth for a thousand years. This millennium is neither part of the present age nor of the world to come (to which John devotes chapters 21–22). It is transitional. The saints have been resurrected, and yet death has not yet been destroyed (see Paul in 1 Cor. 15:26, "the last enemy to be destroyed is death"). The transition is necessary in order to show that just as the Dragon existed before the Beast, the False Prophet, and the prostitute (chap. 12),[15] so he

---

14. This is the view of G. B. Caird, *The Revelation of St. John the Divine*, Harper's New Testament Commentaries (New York: Harper and Row, 1966), 258. Caird says of "Gog and Magog" (20:8), and their destruction with fire from heaven, that John's "emotional attitude to them is very much that of the modern reader of science fiction, who can contemplate with equanimity the liquidation of Mars-men with a ray gun, because they do not belong to the ordered structure of human existence. . . . they come from the four corners of the earth, the outlandish territory beyond the bounds of civilization."

15. Note the formal reintroduction of the Dragon in 20:2, corresponding to his first formal introduction in 12:9.

will be here long after they are gone. But finally he too will be destroyed.

Because the millennial reign is transitional, this view recognizes—or should—that it stands at the far edge of John's horizons, where the sky meets the sea. Its theological contributions to the Book of Revelation are its graphic pictures of the vindication of the martyrs and of Satan's final consignment to the lake of fire. Otherwise, John's interest in it is not for its own sake but as a kind of threshold to his visions of the new world and its new holy city (chaps. 21–22). This is a kind of premillennial view, but one that does not regard the millennium as the key to understanding all of the Revelation.[16]

## Conclusion

The student who has read this far should know by now that there is no single, simple key to understanding the Book of Revelation. All of the Bible, including this book, yields up its treasures only to hard work, prayer, common sense, and a little (not too much!) imagination. The purpose of preaching from the Revelation is to evoke first wonder and then faithfulness to the slain Lamb, not to explain the book away or reduce it to a blueprint of the future. The preacher's task is to stand out of the way and let the book's images do their work.

Of the two "sins" a preacher can commit—to ignore or explain away the Book of Revelation, or to reduce it to a time chart, the first is the more serious. Garrison Keillor tells the story of a prophecy teacher who came every year to Lake Wobegon and explained the whole Bible to the "Sanctified Brethren" with the help of an elaborate chart called "The Course of Time from Eternity to Eternity." The chart revealed everything, from "the world in chaos on the far left to the eternal hereafter on the right."

"When I was a kid," Keillor explains, "I could look at that chart and feel that I understood all of human history. There on the chart

---

16. Merrill C. Tenney's discussion a generation ago of eschatology and the millennium in the Book of Revelation (*Interpreting Revelation* [Grand Rapids: Eerdmans, 1957], 147–67) still has value for the evangelical student today, as does his chapter on the book's christology (117–34).

it was perfectly explained and simplified. This wasn't anything I could have explained to anybody else. It was simply a feeling of utter certainty."

One year the prophecy teacher went out to join the men working in the fields and fainted from sunstroke. When they stripped away his shirt, they were shocked to see that he had a tattoo. "That was his past," Keillor commented, "Yes. That was his mark."[17] Not the mark of the Beast (Rev. 13:16–17), and not the name of the Lamb and of his Father (Rev. 14:1). Just a tattoo. Just a mark of our common humanity.

The prophecy teacher was only a man, possibly with a dubious past, but the time chart was his way of touching eternity and sharing that touch with others. It belonged to his horizons—the horizons of Lake Wobegon and middle America—not necessarily the horizons of Patmos. But at least he tried. As we have seen, even John's horizons were limited. Keillor concluded that "prophecy can explain only so much. Storytelling is required for the rest."[18] Exactly! . . . provided we tell the right story. At the heart of the Book of Revelation *is* a story, the same gospel story that echoes throughout the entire New Testament, about a slain Lamb victorious over death and evil and a God who makes everything new. There is no one correct way to read or preach from the Book of Revelation, but there is one thing we must *not* do. We must never forget that story.

17. "The Wobegon Preacher: An Interview with Garrison Keillor," in *Leadership* 10.4 (Fall 1991): 58–59.

18. Ibid., 59.

# Select Bibliography for the Book of Revelation

Various books and articles, as well as primary sources (for example, apocalyptic literature) have been cited in footnotes throughout this volume. The following list is limited to twenty recent and representative works on the Revelation that the student may want to consult on a fairly regular basis. Because Revelation is a single New Testament book, the list is weighted more toward commentaries than might otherwise be the case.

## Commentaries

Beasley-Murray, George R. *The Book of Revelation.* New Century Bible. London: Oliphants, 1974.

Beckwith, Isbon T. *The Apocalypse of John.* London: Macmillan, 1919.

Boring, M. Eugene. *Revelation.* Interpretation: A Bible Commentary for Teaching and Preaching. Louisville: John Knox, 1989.

Caird, G. B. *A Commentary on the Revelation of St. John the Divine.* Harper's New Testament Commentary. New York: Harper and Row, 1966.

Charles, R. H. *A Critical and Exegetical Commentary on the Revelation of St. John,* 2 vols., International Critical Commentary. Edinburgh: T. and T. Clark, 1920.

Ladd, George E. *A Commentary on the Revelation of John.* Grand Rapids: Eerdmans, 1972.

Mounce, Robert H. *The Book of Revelation.* Grand Rapids: Eerdmans, 1977.

Swete, Henry B. *The Apocalypse of St. John.* London: Macmillan, 1906.

Wall, Robert W. *Revelation*. New International Biblical Commentary. Peabody, Mass.: Hendrickson, 1991.

Walvoord, John F. *The Revelation of Jesus Christ*. Chicago: Moody, 1966.

## Books and Monographs

Aune, David E. *Prophecy in Early Christianity and the Ancient Mediterranean World*. Grand Rapids: Eerdmans, 1983.

Court, John M. *Myth and History in the Book of Revelation*. London: SPCK, 1979.

Farrer, Austin. *A Rebirth of Images: The Making of St. John's Apocalypse*. London: Dacre, 1949.

Hemer, Colin J. *The Letters to the Seven Churches of Asia in their Local Setting*. Sheffield, England: JSOT, 1986.

Hill, David. *New Testament Prophecy*. London: Marshall, Morgan, and Scott, 1979.

Minear, Paul S. *I Saw a New Earth: An Introduction to the Visions of the Apocalypse*. Washington, D.C.: Corpus, 1968.

Schuessler Fiorenza, Elisabeth. *The Book of Revelation. Justice and Judgment*. Philadelphia: Fortress, 1985.

Tenney, Merrill C. *Interpreting Revelation*. Grand Rapids: Eerdmans, 1957.

Thompson, Leonard L. *The Book of Revelation. Apocalypse and Empire*. New York: Oxford University Press, 1990.

Yarbro Collins, Adela. *Crisis and Catharsis: The Power of the Apocalypse*. Louisville: Westminster-John Knox, 1984.

# Interpreting
## the Book
## of Revelation

Guides to New Testament Exegesis
Scot McKnight, General Editor

1. Introducing New Testament Interpretation
2. Interpreting the Synoptic Gospels
3. Interpreting the Gospel of John
4. Interpreting the Book of Acts
5. Interpreting the Pauline Epistles
6. Interpreting the Book of Hebrews (forthcoming)
7. Interpreting the Book of Revelation